Great Jobs
for
Accounting
Majors

Great Jobs
for
Accounting
Majors

Jan Goldberg

SERIES DEVELOPERS AND CONTRIBUTING AUTHORS
Stephen E. Lambert
Julie Ann DeGalan

VGM Career Horizons
NTC/Contemporary Publishing Group

Library of Congress Cataloging-in-Publication Data

Goldberg, Jan.
    Great jobs for accounting majors / Jan Goldberg.
       p.   cm. — (VGM career books)
    Includes index.
    ISBN 0-8442-4744-8
    1. Accounting—Vocational guidance—United States.   I. Title.
II. Series.
    HF5616.U5G643   1998
    657'.023'73—dc21
                                  97-46617
                                       CIP

Material in Appendix C reprinted by permission of the McIntire School of Commerce at the University of Virginia.

Published by VGM Career Horizons
A division of NTC/Contemporary Publishing Group, Inc.
4255 West Touhy Avenue, Lincolnwood (Chicago), Illinois 60646-1975 U.S.A.
Printed in the United States of America
International Standard Book Number: 0-8442-4744-8

18   17   16   15   14   13   12   11   10   9   8   7   6   5   4   3   2   1

Dedication

To the memory of my father and mother, Sam and Sylvia Lefkovitz, and a special aunt, Estelle Lefko, for always encouraging me to follow my dreams.

CONTENTS

Acknowledgments

The author gratefully acknowledges the professionals who graciously agreed to be profiled within this text, as well as the associations and organizations that provided valuable and interesting information.

Thanks to my dear husband, Larry; daughters, Sherri and Debbie; son-in-law, Bruce; sister, Adrienne; and brother, Paul; for their encouragement and support.

Thanks also to family and close friends: Michele, Alison, Steven, Marty, Mindi, Cary, Michele, Marci, Steven, Brian, Jesse, Bertha, Uncle Bernard, and Aunt Helen.

A special thanks to a special friend, Diana Catlin.

Sincere gratitude to Betsy Lancefield, editor of VGM Career Horizons, for providing this challenging opportunity and her help whenever and wherever it is needed.

ACCOUNTING: A DEGREE THAT ADDS UP

"Of all debts—men are least willing to pay the taxes. What a satire is this on government! Everywhere they think they get their money's worth, except for these."

—Ralph Waldo Emerson

Some of the earliest accounting records were written on papyrus and clay tablets in cuneiform and hieroglyphics. Besides ancient picture writing, cuneiform is considered to be the oldest kind of writing in the world, a system invented by the ancient Sumerians around 3000 B.C.

Even the Bible makes mention of accounting, noting that proper accounting between people can lessen arguments and disagreements. Other evidence of accounting practices from approximately 600 B.C. has been credited to ancient Roman businesses and household records. Accounting in China and Asia date back to the very distant past.

Modern accounting dates from fifteenth-century Italy, during the height of trading, when bookkeeping was required to keep track of imports and exports of goods. As new accounting procedures were created and practiced widely, the need for trained professionals soon became apparent.

A guild established in Venice, Italy in the sixteenth century was the first known college of accounting. Training consisted of a six-year apprenticeship program followed by an examination to test the apprentice's knowledge.

Italy remained a leader in accounting until the eighteenth century. From Italy, the practice of accounting spread through Europe to England, and from there to the New World. An accounting society was established in Edinburgh, Scotland in 1854, coinciding with the beginning of the Industrial Revolution. The Industrial Revolution created a need for systematic bookkeeping, which became the primary responsibility of managerial assistants. Sometimes experts were hired to teach the owner of a small business how to keep the books or to verify figures or discover errors in financial records.

In 1887, the first organization of public accountants, The American Association of Public Accountants, was formed. Today it is known as the American Institute of Certified Public Accountants. Ten years after the founding, the state of New York enacted laws setting minimum standards for those engaging in public accounting, and adopted a procedure for licensing. In time, all states passed similar legislation.

Passage of the Sixteenth Amendment to the U.S. Constitution in 1913 provided for taxation of income. Accountants began to prepare income tax returns, becoming authorities on ever-changing regulations and advising individuals and businesses on tax matters. Eventually they began to advise individuals and businesses on financial planning for the future, one of the most important responsibilities they hold to this day.

THE IMPORTANCE OF EDUCATION

While it is true that having a college degree will not guarantee you a position in the world of accounting (or any other field, for that matter), it is important to realize that this is the best way to prepare yourself for and increase your opportunities in the job market. Most employers will not even consider you for a position if you are lacking a four-year degree in accounting or a related field. No matter what career you choose, a higher education will

- ❑ offer a broad base of knowledge and experiences

- ❑ allow you to increase and perfect your skills

- ❑ provide you with opportunities to gain important personal and professional contacts

- ❑ give you the information you need to make an informed career decision

Because multitudes of talented individuals compete for each job opening, you must somehow set yourself above the others. You may accomplish this by combining a college degree with at least one internship, additional formal training or study, experience working in the field, enthusiasm, and a positive attitude.

Good luck in your quest!

PART ONE

THE JOB SEARCH

CHAPTER ONE

THE
SELF-ASSESSMENT

Self-assessment is the process by which you begin to acknowledge your own particular blend of education, experiences, values, needs, and goals. It provides the foundation for career planning and the entire job search process. Self-assessment involves looking inward and asking yourself what can sometimes prove to be difficult questions. This self-examination should lead to an intimate understanding of your personal traits, your personal values, your consumption patterns and economic needs, your longer-term goals, your skill base, your preferred skills, and your under-developed skills.

You come to the self-assessment process knowing yourself well in some of these areas, but you may still be uncertain about other aspects. You may be well aware of your consumption patterns, but have you spent much time specifically identifying your longer-term goals, or your personal values as they relate to work? No matter what level of self-assessment you have undertaken to date, it is now time to clarify all of these issues and questions as they relate to the job search.

The knowledge you gain in the self-assessment process will guide the rest of your job search. In this book, you will learn about all of the following tasks:

- ❑ Writing resumes

- ❑ Exploring possible job titles

- ❑ Identifying employment sites

- ❑ Networking

- ❑ Interviewing

- ❑ Following up

- ❑ Evaluating job offers

In each of these steps, you will rely on and return often to the understanding gained through your self-assessment. Any individual seeking employment must be able and willing to express to potential recruiters and interviewers throughout the job search these facets of his or her personality. This communication allows you to show the world who you are so that together with employers you can determine whether there will be a workable match with a given job or career path.

HOW TO CONDUCT A SELF-ASSESSMENT

The self-assessment process goes on naturally all the time. People ask you to clarify what you mean, or you make a purchasing decision, or you begin a new relationship. You react to the world and the world reacts to you. How you understand these interactions and any changes you might make because of them are part of the natural process of self-discovery. There is, however, a more comprehensive and efficient way to approach self-assessment with regard to employment.

Because self-assessment can become a complex exercise, we have distilled it into a seven-step process that provides an effective basis for undertaking a job search. The seven steps include the following:

1. Understanding your personal traits

2. Identifying your personal values

3. Calculating your economic needs

4. Exploring your longer-term goals

5. Enumerating your skill base

6. Recognizing your preferred skills

7. Assessing skills needing further development

As you work through your self-assessment, you might want to create a worksheet similar to the one shown in Exhibit 1.1. Or you might want to keep a journal of the thoughts you have as you undergo this process. There will be many opportunities to revise your self-assessment as you start down the path of seeking a career.

STEP 1   Understanding Your Personal Traits
Each person has a unique personality that he or she brings to the job search process. Gaining a better understanding of your personal traits can help you

Exhibit 1.1

Self-Assessment Worksheet

STEP 1. Understand Your Personal Traits
The personal traits that describe me are:
(Include all of the words that describe you.)

The ten personal traits that most accurately describe me
are: *(List these ten traits.)*

STEP 2. Identify Your Personal Values
Working conditions that are important to me include:
*(List working conditions that would have to exist for you
to accept a position.)*

The values that go along with my working conditions are:
*(Write down the values that correspond to each working
condition.)*

Some additional values I've decided to include are:
*(List those values you identify as you conduct this job
search.)*

STEP 3. Calculate Your Economic Needs
My estimated minimum annual salary requirement is:
*(Write the salary you have calculated based on your
budget.)*

Starting salaries for the positions I'm considering are:
*(List the name of each job you are considering and the
associated starting salary.)*

STEP 4. Explore Your Longer-Term Goals
My thoughts on longer-term goals right now are:
*(Jot down some of your longer-term goals as you know
them right now.)*

continued

continued

STEP 5. Enumerate Your Skill Base
The general skills I possess are: *(List the skills that underlie tasks you are able to complete.)*

The specific skills I possess are:
(List more technical or specific skills that you possess and indicate your level of expertise.)

General and specific skills that I want to promote to employers for the jobs I'm considering are:
(List general and specific skills for each type of job you are considering.)

STEP 6. Recognize Your Preferred Skills
Skills that I would like to use on the job include:
(List skills that you hope to use on the job, and indicate how often you'd like to use them.)

STEP 7. Assess Skills Needing Further Development
Some skills that I'll need to acquire for the jobs I'm considering include:
(Write down skills listed in job advertisements or job descriptions that you don't currently possess.)

I believe I can build these skills by:
(Describe how you plan to acquire these skills.)

evaluate job and career choices. Identifying these traits, then finding employment that allows you to draw on at least some of them can create a rewarding and fulfilling work experience. If potential employment doesn't allow you to use these preferred traits, it is important to decide whether you can find other ways to express them or whether you would be better off not considering this type of job. Interests and hobbies pursued outside of work hours can be one way to use personal traits you don't have an opportunity to draw on in your work. For example, if you consider yourself an outgoing person and the kinds of jobs you are examining allow little contact with other people, you may be able to achieve the level of interaction that is comfortable for you outside of your work setting. If such a compromise seems impractical or otherwise unsatisfactory, you probably should explore only jobs that provide the interaction you want and need on the job.

Many young adults who are not very confident about their attractiveness to employers will downplay their need for income. They will say, "Money is not all that important if I love my work." But if you begin to document exactly what you need for housing, transportation, insurance, clothing, food, and utilities, you will begin to understand that some jobs cannot meet your financial needs and it doesn't matter how wonderful the job is. If you have to worry each payday about bills and other financial obligations, you won't be very effective on the job. Begin now to be honest with yourself about your needs.

Inventorying Your Personal Traits. Begin the self-assessment process by creating an inventory of your personal traits. Using the list in Exhibit 1.2, decide which of these personal traits describe you.

Exhibit 1.2		
Accurate	Cooperative	Flexible
Active	Courageous	Formal
Adaptable	Critical	Friendly
Adventurous	Curious	Future-oriented
Affectionate	Daring	Generous
Aggressive	Decisive	Gentle
Ambitious	Deliberate	Good-natured
Analytical	Detail-oriented	Helpful
Appreciative	Determined	Honest
Artistic	Discreet	Humorous
Brave	Dominant	Idealistic
Businesslike	Eager	Imaginative
Calm	Easygoing	Impersonal
Capable	Efficient	Independent
Caring	Emotional	Individualistic
Cautious	Empathetic	Industrious
Cheerful	Energetic	Informal
Clean	Excitable	Innovative
Competent	Expressive	Intellectual
Confident	Extroverted	Intelligent
Conscientious	Fair-minded	Introverted
Conservative	Farsighted	Intuitive
Considerate	Feeling	Inventive
Cool	Firm	continued

continued

Jovial	Pleasant	Sensible
Just	Poised	Sensitive
Kind	Polite	Serious
Liberal	Practical	Sincere
Likable	Precise	Sociable
Logical	Principled	Spontaneous
Loyal	Private	Strong
Mature	Productive	Strong-minded
Methodical	Progressive	Structured
Meticulous	Quick	Subjective
Modest	Quiet	Tactful
Motivated	Rational	Thorough
Objective	Realistic	Thoughtful
Observant	Receptive	Tolerant
Open-minded	Reflective	Trusting
Opportunistic	Relaxed	Trustworthy
Optimistic	Reliable	Truthful
Organized	Reserved	Understanding
Original	Resourceful	Unexcitable
Outgoing	Responsible	Uninhibited
Patient	Reverent	Verbal
Peaceable	Self-confident	Versatile
Personable	Self-controlled	Wholesome
Persuasive	Self-disciplined	Wise

Focusing on Selected Personal Traits. Of all the traits you identified from the list in Exhibit 1.2, select the ten you believe most accurately describe you. If you are having a difficult time deciding, think about which words people who know you well would use to describe you. Keep track of these ten traits.

Considering Your Personal Traits in the Job Search Process. As you begin exploring jobs and careers, watch for matches between your personal traits and the job descriptions you read. Some jobs will require many personal traits you know you possess, and others will not seem to match those traits.

．．．．．．．．．．．．．．．．．．．．．．．．．．．．．．．．

For example, a management accountant can work for a large corporation, requiring the ability to work as part of a team in coordinating schedules and activities with other departments and supervisors. Excellent organizational and interpersonal skills are essential qualities for someone in this position. Self-employed public accountants, on the other hand, usually work alone, interacting only with clients. Both often have deadlines to meet, but the public accountant has far fewer people to answer to and must be able to work independently.

....

Your ability to respond to changing conditions, decision-making ability, productivity, creativity, and verbal skills all have a bearing on your success in and enjoyment of your work life. To better guarantee success, be sure to take the time needed to understand these traits in yourself.

STEP 2 Identifying Your Personal Values

Your personal values affect every aspect of your life, including employment, and they develop and change as you move through life. Values can be defined as principles that we hold in high regard, qualities that are important and desirable to us. Some values aren't ordinarily connected to work (love, beauty, marriage, family, or religion), and others are (autonomy, cooperation, effectiveness, achievement, knowledge, and security). Our values determine, in part, the level of satisfaction we feel in a particular job.

Defining Acceptable Working Conditions. One facet of employment is the set of working conditions that must exist for someone to consider taking a job.

Each of us would probably create a unique list of acceptable working conditions, but items that might be included on many people's lists are the amount of money you would need to be paid, how far you are willing to drive or travel, the amount of freedom you want in determining your own schedule, whether you would be working with people or data or things, and the types of tasks you would be willing to do. Your conditions might include statements of working conditions you will *not* accept; for example, you might not be willing to work at night or on weekends or holidays.

If you were offered a job tomorrow, what conditions would have to exist for you to realistically consider accepting the position? Take some time and make a list of these conditions.

Realizing Associated Values. Your list of working conditions can be used to create an inventory of your values relating to jobs and careers you are exploring. For example, if one of your conditions stated that you wanted to earn at least $25,000 per year, the associated value would be financial gain. If

---

Exhibit 1.3

Work Values

Achievement	Development	Physical activity
Advancement	Effectiveness	Power
Adventure	Excitement	Precision
Attainment	Fast pace	Prestige
Authority	Financial gain	Privacy
Autonomy	Helping	Profit
Belonging	Humor	Recognition
Challenge	Improvisation	Risk
Change	Independence	Security
Communication	Influencing others	Self-expression
Community	Intellectual stimulation	Solitude
Competition	Interaction	Stability
Completion	Knowledge	Status
Contribution	Leading	Structure
Control	Mastery	Supervision
Cooperation	Mobility	Surroundings
Creativity	Moral fulfillment	Time freedom
Decision-making	Organization	Variety

---

another condition was that you wanted to work with a friendly group of people, the value that goes along with that might be belonging or interaction with people. Exhibit 1.3 provides a list of commonly held values that relate to the work environment; use it to create your own list of personal values.

Relating Your Values to the World of Work. As you read the job descriptions in this book and in other suggested resources, think about the values associated with that position.

• •

For example, the duties of an Internal Revenue Service agent would include researching, investigating, and conducting interviews; organizing information in a logical format; and writing and editing reports. Associated values are organization, precision, communication, and decision making.

• •

If you were thinking about a career in this field, or any other field you're exploring, at least some of the associated values should match those you extracted from your list of working conditions. Take a second look at any values that don't match up. How important are they to you? What will happen if they are not satisfied on the job? Can you incorporate those personal values elsewhere? Your answers need to be brutally honest. As you continue your exploration, be sure to add to your list any additional values that occur to you.

STEP 3 Calculating Your Economic Needs

Each of us grew up in an environment that provided for certain basic needs, such as food and shelter, and, to varying degrees, other needs that we now consider basic, such as cable TV, reading materials, or an automobile. Needs such as privacy, space, and quiet, which at first glance may not appear to be monetary needs, may add to housing expenses and so should be considered as you examine your economic needs. For example, if you place a high value on a large, open living space for yourself, it would be difficult to satisfy that need without an associated high housing cost, especially in a densely populated city environment.

As you prepare to move into the world of work and become responsible for meeting your own basic needs, it is important to consider the salary you will need to be able to afford a satisfying standard of living. The three-step process outlined here will help you plan a budget, which in turn will allow you to evaluate the various career choices and geographic locations you are considering. The steps include (1) developing a realistic budget, (2) examining starting salaries, and (3) using a cost-of-living index.

Developing a Realistic Budget. Each of us has certain expectations for the kind of lifestyle we want to maintain. In order to begin the process of defining your economic needs, it will be helpful to determine what you expect to spend on routine monthly expenses. These expenses include housing, food, transportation, entertainment, utilities, loan repayments, and revolving charge accounts. A worksheet that details many of these expenses is shown in Exhibit 1.4. You may not currently spend for certain items, but you probably will

---

Exhibit 1.4

Estimated Monthly Expenses Worksheet

		Could Reduce Spending? (Yes/No)
Cable	$ _____	_____
Child care	_____	_____

continued

continued

		Could Reduce Spending? (Yes/No)
Clothing	_____	_____
Educational loan repayment	_____	_____
Entertainment	_____	_____
Food	_____	_____
At home	_____	_____
Meals out	_____	_____
Gifts	_____	_____
Housing		
Rent/mortgage	_____	_____
Insurance	_____	_____
Property taxes	_____	_____
Medical insurance	_____	_____
Reading materials		
Newspapers	_____	_____
Magazines	_____	_____
Books	_____	_____
Revolving loans/charges	_____	_____
Savings	_____	_____
Telephone	_____	_____
Transportation		
Auto payment	_____	_____
Insurance	_____	_____
Parking	_____	_____
—or		
Cab/train/bus fare	_____	_____
Utilities		
Electric	_____	_____
Gas	_____	_____
Water/sewer	_____	_____
Vacations	_____	_____
Miscellaneous expense 1	_____	_____
Expense: _____		
Miscellaneous expense 2	_____	_____
Expense: _____		
Miscellaneous expense 3	_____	_____
Expense: _____		

TOTAL MONTHLY EXPENSES: _____

YEARLY EXPENSES (Monthly expenses x 12): _____

INCREASE TO INCLUDE TAXES (Yearly expenses x 1.35):_____ =

MINIMUM ANNUAL SALARY REQUIREMENT _____

have to once you begin supporting yourself. As you develop this budget, be generous in your estimates, but keep in mind any items that could be reduced or eliminated. If you are not sure about the cost of a certain item, talk with family or friends who would be able to give you a realistic estimate.

If this is new or difficult for you, start to keep a log of expenses right now. You may be surprised at how much you actually spend each month for food or stamps or magazines. Household expenses and personal grooming items can often loom very large in a budget, as can auto repairs or home maintenance.

Income taxes must also be taken into consideration when examining salary requirements. State and local taxes vary by location, so it is difficult to calculate exactly the effect of taxes on the amount of income you need to generate. To roughly estimate the gross income necessary to generate your minimum annual salary requirement, multiply the minimum salary you have calculated (see Exhibit 1.4) by a factor of 1.35. The resulting figure will be an approximation of what your gross income would need to be, given your estimated expenses.

Examining Starting Salaries. Starting salaries for each of the career tracks are provided throughout this book. These salary figures can be used in conjunction with the cost-of-living index (discussed in the next section) to determine whether you would be able to meet your basic economic needs in a given geographic location.

Using a Cost-of-Living Index. If you are thinking about trying to get a job in a geographic region other than the one where you now live, understanding differences in the cost of living will help you come to a more informed decision about making a move. By using a cost-of-living index, you can compare salaries offered and the cost of living in different locations with what you know about the salaries offered and the cost of living in your present location.

Many variables are used to calculate the cost-of-living index, including housing expenses, groceries, utilities, transportation, health care, clothing, entertainment, local income taxes, and local sales taxes. Cost-of-living indices can be found in many resources, such as *Equal Employment Opportunity Bimonthly, Places Rated Almanac,* or *The Best Towns in America.* They are constantly being recalculated based on changes in costs.

· ·

If you lived in Cleveland, Ohio, for example, and you were interested in working as a high school accounting teacher in the Cleveland School District, you would earn, on average, $21,093 annually. But let's say you're thinking about moving to either New York, Los Angeles, or Minneapolis.

You know you can live on $21,093 in Cleveland, but you want to be able to equal that salary in other locations you're considering. How much will you need to earn in those locations to do this? Figuring the cost of living for each city will show you.

Job: High School Accounting Teacher

CITY	INDEX	EQUIVALENT SALARY

$$\frac{\text{New York}}{\text{Cleveland}} \quad \frac{213.3}{114.3} \times \$21,093 = \$39,363 \text{ in New York}$$

$$\frac{\text{Los Angeles}}{\text{Cleveland}} \quad \frac{124.6}{114.3} \times \$21,093 = \$22,994 \text{ in Los Angeles}$$

$$\frac{\text{Minneapolis}}{\text{Cleveland}} \quad \frac{100.0}{114.3} \times \$21,093 = \$19,303 \text{ in Minneapolis}$$

Let's walk through this example. In any cost-of-living index, the number 100 represents the national average cost of living, and each city is assigned an index number based on current prices in that city for the items included in the index (housing, food, etc.). In the index we used, New York was assigned the number 213.3, Los Angeles' index was 124.6, Minneapolis' was 100.0, and Cleveland's index was 114.3. In other words, it costs more than twice as much to live in New York as it does in Minneapolis. We can set up a table to determine exactly how much you would have to earn in each of these cities to have the same buying power that you have in Cleveland.

You would have to earn $39,363 in New York, $22,994 in Los Angeles, and $19,303 in Minneapolis to match the buying power of $21,093 in Cleveland.

If you would like to determine whether it's financially worthwhile to make any of these moves, one more piece of information is needed: the salaries of high school accounting teachers in these other cities. The Association for School, College, and University Staffing, Inc. reports the following average salary information for elementary and secondary school teachers in the 1995–1996 school year:

Region	Annual Salary	Salary Equivalent to Ohio	Change in Buying Power
Mid Atlantic (including New York)	$23,751	$39,363	–$15,612
West (including Los Angeles)	$24,447	$22,994	+$1,453
Great Plains (including Minneapolis)	$20,068	$19,303	+$765
Midwest (including Cleveland)	$21,093	—	—

If you moved to New York City and secured employment as a high school accounting teacher, you would not be able to maintain a lifestyle similar to the one you led in Cleveland; in fact, you would have to add more than 50 percent to your income to maintain a similar lifestyle in New York. The same would not be true for a move to Los Angeles or Minneapolis. You would increase your buying power given the rate of pay and cost of living in these cities.

••

You can work through a similar exercise for any type of job you are considering and for many locations when current salary information is available. It will be worth your time to undertake this analysis if you are seriously considering a relocation. By doing so you will be able to make an informed choice.

STEP 4   Exploring Your Longer-Term Goals

There is no question that when we first begin working, our goals are to use our skills and education in a job that will reward us with employment, income, and status relative to the preparation we brought with us to this position. If we are not being paid as much as we feel we should for our level of education, or if job demands don't provide the intellectual stimulation we had hoped for, we experience unhappiness and, as a result, often seek other employment.

Most jobs we consider "good" are those that fulfill our basic "lower-level" needs of security, food, clothing, shelter, income, and productive work. But even when our basic needs are met and our jobs are secure and productive, we as individuals are constantly changing. As we change, the demands and expectations we place on our jobs may change. Fortunately, some jobs grow and change with us, and this explains why some people are happy throughout many years in a job.

But more often people are bigger than the jobs they fill. We have more goals and needs than any job could fulfill. These are "higher-level" needs of self-esteem, companionship, affection, and an increasing desire to feel we are employing ourselves in the most effective way possible. Not all of these higher-level needs can be fulfilled through employment, but for as long as we are employed, we increasingly demand that our jobs play their part in moving us along the path to fulfillment.

Another obvious but important fact is that we change as we mature. Although our jobs also have the potential for change, they may not change as frequently or as markedly as we do. There are increasingly fewer one-job, one-employer careers; we must think about a work future that may involve voluntary or forced moves from employer to employer. Because of that very real possibility, we need to take advantage of the opportunities in each position we hold to acquire skills and competencies that will keep us viable and attractive as employees in a job market that is not only increasingly technology/computer dependent, but also is populated with more and more small, self-transforming organizations rather than the large, seemingly stable organizations of the past.

It may be difficult in the early stages of the job search to determine whether the path you are considering can meet these longer-term goals. Reading about career paths and individual career histories in your field can be very helpful in this regard. Meeting and talking with individuals further along in their careers can be enlightening as well. Older workers can provide valuable guidance on "self-managing" your career, which will become an increasingly valuable skill in the future. Some of these ideas may seem remote as you read this now, but you should be able to appreciate the need to ensure that you are growing, developing valuable new skills, and researching other employers who might be interested in your particular skills package.

....

If you are considering a position as an IRS agent, you will gain a better perspective on this career by talking to employees in different divisions (e.g., Examination, Collections, and Criminal Investigation) who hold different levels of responsibility: an entry-level field employee, a more experienced revenue agent, and finally a supervisor or division head who has a considerable work history with the IRS. Each will have a different perspective, unique concerns, and an individual set of priorities.

....

STEP 5 Enumerating Your Skill Base

In terms of the job search, skills can be thought of as capabilities that can be developed in school, at work, or by volunteering and then used in specific job settings. Many studies have documented the kinds of skills that employers seek in entry-level applicants. For example, some of the most desired skills for individuals interested in the teaching profession include the ability to interact effectively with students one on one, to manage a classroom, to adapt to varying situations as necessary, and to get involved in school activities. Business employers have also identified important qualities, including enthusiasm for the employer's product or service, a businesslike mind, the ability to follow written or verbal instructions, the ability to demonstrate self-control, the confidence to suggest new ideas, the ability to communicate with all members of a group, awareness of cultural differences, and loyalty, to name just a few. You will find that many of these skills are also in the repertoire of qualities demanded in your college major.

In order to be successful in obtaining any given job, you must be able to demonstrate that you possess a certain mix of skills that will allow you to carry out the duties required by that job. This skill mix will vary a great deal from job to job; to determine the skills necessary for the jobs you are seeking, you can read job advertisements or more generic job descriptions, such as those found later in this book. If you want to be effective in the job search, you must directly show employers that you possess the skills needed to be successful in filling the position. These skills will initially be described on your resume and then discussed again during the interview process.

Skills are either general or specific. General skills are those that are developed throughout the college years by taking classes, being employed, and getting involved in other related activities such as volunteer work or campus organizations. General skills include the ability to read and write, to perform computations, to think critically, and to communicate effectively. Specific skills are also acquired on the job and in the classroom, but they allow you to complete tasks that require specialized knowledge. Computer programming, drafting, language translating, and copyediting are just a few examples of specific skills that may relate to a given job.

In order to develop a list of skills relevant to employers, you must first identify the general skills you possess, then list specific skills you have to offer, and, finally, examine which of these skills employers are seeking.

Identifying Your General Skills. Because you possess or will possess a college degree, employers will assume that you can read and write, perform certain basic computations, think critically, and communicate effectively. Employers will want to see that you have acquired these skills, and they will want to know which additional general skills you possess.

One way to begin identifying skills is to write an experiential diary. An experiential diary lists all the tasks you were responsible for completing for each job you've held and then outlines the skills required to do those tasks. You may list several skills for any given task. This diary allows you to distinguish between the tasks you performed and the underlying skills required to complete those tasks. Here's an example:

Tasks	Skills
Answering telephone	Effective use of language, clear diction, ability to direct inquiries, ability to solve problems
Waiting on tables	Poise under conditions of time and pressure, speed, accuracy, good memory, simultaneous completion of tasks, sales skills

For each job or experience you have participated in, develop a worksheet based on the example shown here. On a resume, you may want to describe these skills rather than simply listing tasks. Skills are easier for the employer to appreciate, especially when your experience is very different from the employment you are seeking. In addition to helping you identify general skills, this experiential diary will prepare you to speak more effectively in an interview about the qualifications you possess.

Identifying Your Specific Skills. It may be easier to identify your specific skills, because you can definitely say whether you can speak other languages, program a computer, draft a map or diagram, or edit a document using appropriate symbols and terminology.

Using your experiential diary, identify the points in your history where you learned how to do something very specific, and decide whether you have a beginning, intermediate, or advanced knowledge of how to use that particular skill. Right now, be sure to list *every* specific skill you have, and don't consider whether you like using the skill. Write down a list of specific skills you have acquired and the level of competence you possess—beginning, intermediate, or advanced.

Relating Your Skills to Employers. You probably have thought about a couple of different jobs you might be interested in obtaining, and one way to begin relating the general and specific skills you possess to potential employer needs is to read actual advertisements for these types of positions (see Part II for resources listing actual job openings).

For example, you might be interested in a career as an auditor. A typical job listing might read, "Requires 2 to 5 years' experience, organizational and interpersonal skills, analytical ability, drive, and the ability to work under pressure." You could find more information in a general source that describes the job of an auditor, where you would learn that auditors also design internal control systems, analyze financial data, work with statistics, and must be thoroughly knowledgeable of computer information systems.

Begin building a comprehensive list of required skills with the first job description you read. Exploring advertisements for and descriptions of several types of related positions will reveal an important core of skills necessary for obtaining the type of work you're interested in. In building this list, include both general and specific skills.

Following is a sample list of skills needed to be successful as an auditor. These items were extracted from general resources and actual job listings.

Job: Auditor

General Skills	Specific Skills
Ability to gather and interpret information	Write memos
	Write financial reports
Possession of a specific body of knowledge	Edit reports
	Monitor information systems
Familiarity with computer systems	Master various software
Ability to work independently	Deliver oral reports
Ability to work well with other people	Design control systems
	Calculate taxes
Strong written and verbal skills	Investigate mismanagement
Organizational skills	Provide advice to clients
Integrity	

On separate sheets of paper, try to generate a comprehensive list of required skills for at least one job you are considering. The list of general skills that you develop for a given career path will be valuable for any number of jobs you might apply for. Many of the specific skills will also be transferable to other positions. For example, the ability to understand a business system to investigate the possibility of mismanagement would be a required skill not only for auditors but also for management consultants.

· ·

Now review the list of skills you developed and check off those skills that you *know you possess* and that are required for jobs you are considering. You should refer to these specific skills on the resume that you write for this type of job. See Chapter 2 for details on resume writing.

STEP 6 Recognizing Your Preferred Skills

In the previous section, you developed a comprehensive list of skills that relate to particular career paths that are of interest to you. You can now relate these to skills that you prefer to use. We all use a wide range of skills (some researchers say individuals have a repertoire of about 500 skills), but we may not be particularly interested in using all of them in our work. There may be some skills that come to us more naturally or that we use successfully time and time again and that we want to continue to use; these are best described as our preferred skills. For this exercise, use the list of skills that you developed for the previous section and decide which of them you are *most interested in using* in future work and how often you would like to use them. You might be interested in using some skills only occasionally, while others you would like to use more regularly. You probably also have skills that you hope you can use constantly.

As you examine job announcements, look for matches between this list of preferred skills and the qualifications described in the advertisements. These skills should be highlighted on your resume and discussed in job interviews.

STEP 7 Assessing Skills Needing Further Development

Previously you developed a list of general and specific skills required for given positions. You already possess some of these skills; those that remain to be developed are your underdeveloped skills.

If you are just beginning the job search, there may be gaps between the qualifications required for some of the jobs being considered and skills you possess. These are your underdeveloped skills. The thought of having to admit to and talk about these underdeveloped skills, especially in a job interview, is a frightening one. One way to put a healthy perspective on this subject is to target and relate your exploration of underdeveloped skills to the types of positions you are seeking. Recognizing these shortcomings and planning to overcome them with either on-the-job training or additional formal education can be a positive way to address the concept of underdeveloped skills.

On your worksheet or in your journal, make a list of up to five general or specific skills required for the positions you're interested in that you *don't currently possess*. For each item, list an idea you have for specific action you could take to acquire that skill. Do some brainstorming to come up with possible actions. If you have a hard time generating ideas, talk to people currently working in this type of position, professionals in your college career services office, trusted friends, family members, or members of related professional associations.

If, for example, you are interested in a job for which you don't have some specific required experience, you could locate training opportunities such as classes or workshops offered through a local college or university, community college, or club or association that would help you build the level of expertise you need for the job.

Many excellent jobs in today's economy demand computer skills you probably already have. Most graduates are not so lucky, and have to acquire these skills—often before an employer will give their application serious consideration. So, what can you do if you find there are certain skills you're missing? If you're still in school, try to fill the gaps in your knowledge before you graduate. If you've already graduated, look at evening programs, continuing education courses, or tutorial programs that may be available commercially. Developing a modest level of expertise will encourage you to be more confident in suggesting to potential employers that you can continue to add to your skill base on the job.

In Chapter 5 on interviewing, we will discuss in detail how to effectively address questions about underdeveloped skills. Generally speaking, though, employers want genuine answers to these types of questions. They want you to reveal "the real you," and they also want to see how you answer difficult questions. In taking the positive, targeted approach discussed above, you show the employer that you are willing to continue to learn and that you have a plan for strengthening your job qualifications.

USING YOUR SELF-ASSESSMENT

Exploring entry-level career options can be an exciting experience if you have good resources available and will take the time to use them. Can you effectively complete the following tasks?

1. Understand and relate your personality traits to career choices

2. Define your personal values

3. Determine your economic needs

4. Explore longer-term goals

5. Understand your skill base

6. Recognize your preferred skills

7. Express a willingness to improve on your underdeveloped skills

If so, then you can more meaningfully participate in the job search process by writing a more effective resume, finding job titles that represent work you are interested in doing, locating job sites that will provide the opportunity for you to use your strengths and skills, networking in an informed way, participating in focused interviews, getting the most out of follow-up contacts, and evaluating job offers to find those that create a good match between you and the employer. The remaining chapters guide you through these next steps in the job search process. For many job seekers, this process can take anywhere from three months to a year to implement. The time you will need to put into your job search will depend on the type of job you want and the geographic location where you'd like to work. Think of your effort as a job in itself, requiring you to set aside time each week to complete the needed work. Carefully undertaken efforts may reduce the time you need for your job search.

CHAPTER TWO

THE RESUME AND COVER LETTER

The task of writing a resume may seem overwhelming if you are unfamiliar with this type of document, but there are some easily understood techniques that can and should be used. This section was written to help you understand the purpose of the resume, the different types of resume formats available, and how to write the sections of information traditionally found on a resume. We will present examples and explanations that address questions frequently posed by people writing their first resume or updating an old resume.

Even within the formats and suggestions given below, however, there are infinite variations. True, most resumes follow one of the outlines suggested below, but you should feel free to adjust the resume to suit your needs and make it expressive of your life and experience.

WHY WRITE A RESUME?

The purpose of a resume is to convince an employer that you should be interviewed. You'll want to present enough information to show that you can make an immediate and valuable contribution to an organization. A resume is not an in-depth historical or legal document; later in the job search process you'll be asked to document your entire work history on an application form and attest to its validity. The resume should, instead, highlight relevant information pertaining directly to the organization that will receive the document or the type of position you are seeking.

We will discuss four types of resumes in this chapter: chronological resume, functional resume, targeted resume, and the broadcast letter. The reasons for using one type of resume over another and the typical format for each are addressed in the following sections.

THE CHRONOLOGICAL RESUME

The chronological resume is the most common of the various resume formats and therefore the format that employers are most used to receiving. This type of resume is easy to read and understand because it details the chronological progression of jobs you have held. (See Exhibit 2.1.) It begins with your most recent employment and works back in time. If you have a solid work history, or experience that provided growth and development in your duties and responsibilities, a chronological resume will highlight these achievements. The typical elements of a chronological resume include the heading, a career objective, educational background, employment experience, activities, and references.

The Heading

The heading consists of your name, address, and telephone number. Recently it has come to include fax numbers and electronic mail addresses as well. We suggest that you spell out your full name and type it in all capital letters in bold type. After all, you are the focus of the resume! If you have a current as well as a permanent address and you include both in the heading, be sure to indicate until what date your current address will be valid. Don't forget to include the zip code with your address and the area code with your telephone number.

The Objective

As you formulate the wording for this part of your resume, keep the following points in mind.

The Objective Focuses the Resume. Without a doubt, this is the most challenging part of the resume for most resume writers. Even for individuals who have quite firmly decided on a career path, it can be difficult to encapsulate all they want to say in one or two brief sentences. For job seekers who are unfocused or unclear about their intentions, trying to write this section can inhibit the entire resume writing process.

Recruiters tell us, time and again, that the objective creates a frame of reference for them. It helps them see how you express your goals and career focus.

Exhibit 2.1

Chronological Resume

ANN PARKER

3400 El Camino Real
Boca Raton, FL 33432
(561) 555-7890

OBJECTIVE

A career as a management accountant for a large corporation or healthcare facility, ultimately working with internal auditing.

EDUCATION

Bachelor of Arts in accounting
Florida Atlantic University
Boca Raton, Florida
May 1998
Overall GPA 3.2 on a 4.0 scale

RELATED COURSES

Information Systems Design	Financial Analysis
Cost Accounting	Management Analysis

EXPERIENCE

Internship
Motorola Corporation
Fort Lauderdale, Florida
1997 to present
Assistant to the Associate Financial Director
Examined financial records, wrote reports

Summer Work-Study
Boca Raton Community Hospital
Summers, 1995 to 1997
Bookkeeping department—assisted with payroll and withholding tax deductions

PORTFOLIO

Portfolio of projects completed during the internship is available upon request.

continued

---

continued

COMMUNITY SERVICE
Volunteer, Medical Records Department, North Broward General Hospital; Intake Processor, Student Red Cross Blood Drive (two years), Florida Atlantic University

REFERENCES
Personal and professional references are available upon request.

In addition, the statement may indicate in what ways you can immediately benefit an organization. Given the importance of the objective, every point covered in the resume should relate to it. If information doesn't relate, it should be omitted. With the word processing technology available today, each resume can and should be tailored for individual employers or specific positions that are available.

Choose an Appropriate Length. Because of the brevity necessary for a resume, you should keep the objective as short as possible. Although objectives of only four or five words often don't show much direction, objectives that take three full lines would be viewed as too wordy and might be ignored.

Consider Which Type of Objective Statement You Will Use. There are many ways to state an objective, but generally there are four forms this statement can take: (1) a very general statement; (2) a statement focused on a specific position; (3) a statement focused on a specific industry; or (4) a summary of your qualifications. In our contacts with employers, we often hear that many resumes don't exhibit any direction or career goals, so we suggest avoiding general statements when possible.

1. General Objective Statement. General objective statements look like the following:

- ❑ An entry-level educational programming coordinator position
- ❑ An entry-level marketing position

This type of objective would be useful if you know what type of job you want but you're not sure which industries interest you.

2. Position-Focused Objective. Following are examples of objectives focusing on a specific position:

- ❑ To obtain the position of Conference Coordinator at State College
- ❑ To obtain a position as Assistant Editor at *Time* magazine

When a student applies for an advertised job opening, this type of focus can be very effective. The employer knows that the applicant has taken the time to tailor the resume specifically for this position.

3. Industry-Focused Objective. Focusing on a particular industry in an objective could be stated as follows:

❑ To begin a career as a sales representative in the cruise line industry

4. Summary of Qualifications Statement. The summary of qualifications can be used instead of an objective or in conjunction with an objective. The purpose of this type of statement is to highlight relevant qualifications gained through a variety of experiences. This type of statement is often used by individuals with extensive and diversified work experience. An example of a qualifications statement follows:

··

A degree in accounting and three years of progressively increasing responsibility in the financial department of a local corporation have prepared me for a career as a management accountant in an institution that values hands-on involvement and thoroughness.

··

Support Your Objective. A resume that contains any one of these types of objective statements should then go on to demonstrate why you are qualified to get the position. Listing academic degrees can be one way to indicate qualifications. Another demonstration would be in the way previous experiences, both volunteer and paid, are described. Without this kind of documentation in the body of the resume, the objective looks unsupported. Think of the resume as telling a connected story about you. All the elements should work together to form a coherent picture that ideally should relate to your statement of objective.

Education

This section of your resume should indicate the exact name of the degree you will receive or have received, spelled out completely with no abbreviations. The degree is generally listed after the objective, followed by the institution name and address, and then the month and year of graduation. This section could also include your academic minor, grade point average (GPA), and appearance on the Dean's List or President's List.

If you have enough space, you might want to include a section listing courses related to the field in which you are seeking work. The best use of a "related courses" section would be to list some course work that is not traditionally associated with the major. Perhaps you took several computer courses outside your degree that will be helpful and related to the job prospects you are entertaining. Several education section examples are shown here:

....

- ❑ Bachelor of Science degree in accounting
  Boston University, Boston, Massachusetts, May 1998
  Minor: Human resource management

- ❑ Bachelor of Science degree in accounting
  Tufts University, Medford, Massachusetts, May 1998
  Minor: Computer science

- ❑ Bachelor of Science degree in accounting
  State University, Boulder, Colorado, June 1998
  Minor: Economics

  An example of a format for a related courses section
  follows:

RELATED COURSES	
Corporate Finance	Computer Applications
Economics	Business Research
Real Estate Investment	Design

....

Experience

The experience section of your resume should be the most substantial part and should take up most of the space on the page. Employers want to see what kind of work history you have. They will look at your range of experiences, longevity in jobs, and specific tasks you are able to complete. This section may also be called "work experience," "related experience," "employment history," or "employment." No matter what you call this section, some important points to remember are the following:

1. **Describe your duties** as they relate to the position you are seeking.

2. **Emphasize major responsibilities** and indicate increases in responsibility. Include all relevant employment experiences: summer, part-time, internships, cooperative education, or self-employment.

3. **Emphasize skills,** especially those that transfer from one situation to another. The fact that you coordinated a student organization, chaired meetings, supervised others, and managed a budget leads one to suspect that you could coordinate other things as well.

4. **Use descriptive job titles** that provide information about what you did. A "Student Intern" should be more specifically stated as, for example, "Magazine Operations Intern." "Volunteer" is also too general; a title like "Peer Writing Tutor" would be more appropriate.

5. **Create word pictures** by using active verbs to start sentences. Describe *results* you have produced in the work you have done.

A limp description would say something like the following: "My duties included helping with production, proofreading, and editing. I used a word processing package to alter text." An action statement would be stated as follows: "Coordinated and assisted in the creative marketing of brochures and seminar promotions, becoming proficient in WordPerfect."

Remember, an accomplishment is simply a result, a final measurable product that people can relate to. A duty is not a result, it is an obligation—every job holder has duties. For an effective resume, list as many results as you can. To make the most of the limited space you have and to give your description impact, carefully select appropriate and accurate descriptors from the list of action words in Exhibit 2.2.

Here are some traits that employers tell us they like to see:

❑ Teamwork

❑ Energy and motivation

❑ Learning and using new skills

Exhibit 2.2

Resume Action Verbs

Achieved	Assisted	Communicated
Acted	Attained	Compiled
Administered	Balanced	Completed
Advised	Budgeted	Composed
Analyzed	Calculated	Conceptualized
Assessed	Collected	Condensed

continued

continued

Conducted	Increased	Provided
Consolidated	Influenced	Qualified
Constructed	Informed	Quantified
Controlled	Initiated	Questioned
Converted	Innovated	Realized
Coordinated	Instituted	Received
Corrected	Instructed	Recommended
Created	Integrated	Recorded
Decreased	Interpreted	Reduced
Defined	Introduced	Reinforced
Demonstrated	Learned	Reported
Designed	Lectured	Represented
Determined	Led	Researched
Developed	Maintained	Resolved
Directed	Managed	Reviewed
Documented	Mapped	Scheduled
Drafted	Marketed	Selected
Edited	Met	Served
Eliminated	Modified	Showed
Ensured	Monitored	Simplified
Established	Negotiated	Sketched
Estimated	Observed	Sold
Evaluated	Obtained	Solved
Examined	Operated	Staffed
Explained	Organized	Streamlined
Facilitated	Participated	Studied
Finalized	Performed	Submitted
Generated	Planned	Summarized
Handled	Predicted	Systematized
Headed	Prepared	Tabulated
Helped	Presented	Tested
Identified	Processed	Transacted
Illustrated	Produced	Updated
Implemented	Projected	Verified
Improved	Proposed	

- ❏ Demonstrated versatility

- ❏ Critical thinking

- ❏ Understanding how profits are created

- ❏ Displaying organizational acumen

- ❏ Communicating directly and clearly, in both writing and speaking

- ❏ Risk taking

- ❏ Willingness to admit mistakes

- ❏ Manifesting high personal standards

SOLUTIONS TO FREQUENTLY ENCOUNTERED PROBLEMS

Repetitive Employment with the Same Employer

EMPLOYMENT: **The Foot Locker,** Portland, Oregon. Summer 1991, 1992, 1993. Initially employed in high school as salesclerk. Due to successful performance, asked to return next two summers at higher pay with added responsibility. Ranked as the #2 salesperson the first summer and #1 the next two summers. Assisted in arranging eye-catching retail displays; served as manager of other summer workers during owner's absence.

A Large Number of Jobs

EMPLOYMENT: Recent Hospitality Industry Experience: Affiliated with four upscale hotel/restaurant complexes (September 1991–February 1994), where I worked part- and full-time as a waiter, bartender, disc jockey, and bookkeeper to produce income for college.

Several Positions with the Same Employer

EMPLOYMENT: Coca-Cola Bottling Co., Burlington, VT, 1991–94. In four years, I received three promotions, each with increased pay and responsibility.

Summer Sales Coordinator: Promoted to hire, train, and direct efforts of add-on staff of 15 college-age route salespeople hired to meet summer peak demand for product.

Sales Administrator: Promoted to run home office sales desk, managing accounts and associated delivery schedules for professional sales force of ten people. Intensive phone work, daily interaction with all personnel, and strong knowledge of product line required.

Route Salesperson: Summer employment to travel and tourism industry sites using Coke products. Met specific schedule demands, used good communication skills with wide variety of customers, and demonstrated strong selling skills. Named salesperson of the month for July and August of that year.

QUESTIONS RESUME WRITERS OFTEN ASK

How Far Back Should I Go in Terms of Listing Past Jobs?

Usually, listing three or four jobs should suffice. If you did something back in high school that has a bearing on your future aspirations for employment, by all means list the job. As you progress through your college career, high school jobs may be replaced on the resume by college employment.

Should I Differentiate Between Paid and Nonpaid Employment?

Most employers are not initially as concerned about how much you were paid. They are anxious to know how much responsibility you held in your past employment. There is no need to specify that your work was volunteer if you had significant responsibilities.

How Should I Represent My Accomplishments or Work-Related Responsibilities?

Succinctly, but fully. In other words, give the employer enough information to arouse curiosity, but not so much detail that you leave nothing to the imagination. Besides, some jobs merit more lengthy explanations than others. Be sure to convey any information that can give an employer a better understanding of the depth of your involvement at work. Did you supervise others? How many? Did your efforts result in a more efficient operation? How much did you increase efficiency? Did you handle a budget? How much? Were you promoted in a short time? Did you work two jobs at once or 15 hours per week after high school? Where appropriate, quantify.

Should the Work Section Always Follow the Education Section on the Resume?

Always lead with your strengths. If your education closely relates to the employment you now seek, put this section after the objective. Or, if you are weak on the academic side but have a surplus of good work experiences, consider reversing the order of your sections to lead with employment, followed by education.

How Should I Present My Activities, Honors, Awards, Professional Societies, and Affiliations?

This section of the resume can add valuable information for an employer to consider if used correctly. The rule of thumb for information in this section is to include only those activities that are in some way relevant to the objective stated on your resume. If you can draw a valid connection between your activities and your objective, include them; if not, leave them out.

Granted, this is hard to do. Center on the championship basketball team or coordinator of the biggest homecoming parade ever held are roles that have meaning for you and represent personal accomplishments you'd like to share. But the resume is a brief document, and the information you provide on it should help the employer make a decision about your job eligibility. Including personal details can be confusing and could hurt your candidacy. Limiting your activity list to a few very significant experiences can be very effective.

If you are applying for a position as a safety officer, your certificate in Red Cross lifesaving skills or CPR would be related and valuable. You would want to include it. If, however, you are applying for a job as a junior account executive in an advertising agency, that information would be unrelated and superfluous. Leave it out.

Professional affiliations and honors should *all* be listed; especially important are those related to your job objective. Social clubs and activities need not be a part of your resume unless you hold a significant office or you are looking for a position related to your membership. Be aware that most prospective employers' principle concerns are related to your employability, not your social life. If you have any, publications can be included as an addendum to your resume.

The focus of the resume is your experience and education. It is not necessary to describe your involvement in activities. However, if your resume needs to be lengthened, this section provides the freedom either to expand on or mention only briefly the contributions you have made. If you have made significant contributions (e.g., an officer of an organization or a particularly long tenure with a group), you may choose to describe them in more detail. It is not always necessary to include the dates of your memberships with your activities the way you would include job dates.

There are a number of different ways in which to present additional information. You may give this section a number of different titles. Assess what you want to list, and then use an appropriate title. Do not use extracurricular activities. This terminology is scholastic, not professional, and therefore not appropriate. The following are two examples:

❑ ACTIVITIES: Society for Technical Communication, Student Senate, Student Admissions Representative, Senior Class Officer

❑ ACTIVITIES: • Society for Technical Communication Member
• Student Senator
• Student Admissions Representative
• Senior Class Officer

The position you are looking for will determine what you should or should not include. *Always* look for a correlation between the activity and the prospective job.

How Should I Handle References?

The use of references is considered a part of the interview process, and they should never be listed on a resume. You would always provide references to a potential employer if requested to, so it is not even necessary to include this section on the resume if room does not permit. If space is available, it is acceptable to include one of the following statements:

❑ REFERENCES: Furnished upon request.

❑ REFERENCES: Available upon request.

Individuals used as references must be protected from unnecessary contacts. By including names on your resume, you leave your references unprotected. Overuse and abuse of your references will lead to less-than-supportive comments. Protect your references by giving out their names only when you are being considered seriously as a candidate for a given position.

THE FUNCTIONAL RESUME

The functional resume departs from a chronological resume in that it organizes information by specific accomplishments in various settings: previous jobs, volunteer work, associations, etc. This type of resume permits you to stress the substance of your experiences rather than the position titles you have held. (See Exhibit 2.3.) You should consider using a functional resume if you have held a series of similar jobs that relied on the same skills or abilities.

The Objective

A functional resume begins with an objective that can be used to focus the contents of the resume.

Exhibit 2.3

Functional Resume

GINA BURNS

Broadhurst Hall, Room 310	64 Walnut Avenue
University of Massachusetts	West Newton, MA 02158
Amherst, MA 02245	(617) 555-1325
(408) 555-1222	
(until May 1998)	

OBJECTIVE

An entry-level accounting position in a public accounting firm that allows me to show my initiative and my knowledge of tax law and customer relations.

CAPABILITIES

- Taxation
- Corporate tax programs
- Accounting software programs
- Worker's compensation laws
- Strong people skills

SELECTED ACCOMPLISHMENTS

Accounting: Through my college work-study program I achieved three years of progressively more challenging accounting duties in the payroll department of a local bank. I calculated income tax and FICA withholding, cut checks, kept records, and worked with yearly returns. I also worked for one year in the univerisity financial aid department helping students fill out financial aid forms and loan applications.
Team Player: Collaborated with co-workers and professionals in other bank and university departments including the loan officers, front desk staff, and the university admissions office.

LEADERSHIP

Vice President, National Society of Public Accountants college chapter, 1996 to 1997.

AWARDS

Dean's List (six semesters)

continued

continued
Employee of the month (five times over two years)

EMPLOYMENT HISTORY
First Union Bank of Boston, Amherst, Massachusetts, 1995 to 1998
UMass Financial Aid Office, Amherst, Massachusetts, 1994 to 1995

EDUCATION
Bachelor of Science in accounting
University of Massachusetts, Amherst, Massachusetts
June 1998
I will begin work on my M.B.A. in the fall of 1998, attending night
classes.

REFERENCES
Provided upon request.

Specific Accomplishments

Specific accomplishments are listed on this type of resume. Examples of the types of headings used to describe these capabilities might include sales, counseling, teaching, communication, production, management, marketing, or writing. The headings you choose will directly relate to your experience and the tasks that you carried out. Each accomplishment section contains statements related to your experience in that category, regardless of when or where it occurred. Organize the accomplishments and the related tasks you describe in their order of importance as related to the position you seek.

Experience or Employment History

Your actual work experience is condensed and placed after the specific accomplishments section. It simply lists dates of employment, position titles, and employer names.

Education

The education section of a functional resume is identical to that of the chronological resume, but it does not carry the same visual importance because it is placed near the bottom of the page.

References

Because actual reference names are never listed on a resume, this section is optional if space does not permit.

THE TARGETED RESUME

The targeted resume focuses on specific work-related capabilities you can bring to a given position within an organization. (See Exhibit 2.4.) It should be sent to an individual within the organization who makes hiring decisions about the position you are seeking.

The Objective

The objective on this type of resume should be targeted to a specific career or position. It should be supported by the capabilities, accomplishments, and achievements documented in the resume.

Exhibit 2.4

Targeted Resume

JASON A. DRUMMOND

Jefferson Hall, Room 150
Bevins College
Ann Arbor, MI 86256
(303) 555-0967
(until May 1998)

6789 Congress Avenue
Orlando, FL 32822
(407) 555-3752

JOB TARGET
A position as a field agent with the Internal Revenue Service

CAPABILITIES
- Able to work independently
- Strong quantitative skills
- Familiar with a variety of computer software, including spreadsheets
- Good interviewing skills
- Investigative abilities
- Collect and analyze data

ACHIEVEMENTS
- Created volunteer student team to help senior citizens with income tax preparation
- Successfully completed an internship with a public accounting firm

continued

continued

- Wrote and published several articles in AARP publications on income tax return preparation
- Graduated with honors

WORK HISTORY

1997–1998 Student Internship
H&R Block, Ann Arbor, Michigan
- Completed income tax return forms for private and corporate clients, including royalty income statements and exempt overseas employment

1995–1997 Student Work-Study
Financial Aid office, Bevins College
- Analyzed student financial aid forms in terms of eligibility criteria set by the state

1993–1996 Summer Position (two summers)
Camp Beaverton, Sanbornville, New Hampshire
- Swimming and boating instructor

EDUCATION

1998
Bachelor of Science in accounting
Bevins College, Ann Arbor, Michigan

Capabilities

Capabilities should be statements that illustrate tasks you believe you are capable of based on your accomplishments, achievements, and work history. Each should relate to your targeted career or position. You can stress your qualifications rather than your employment history. This approach may require research to obtain an understanding of the nature of the work involved and the capabilities necessary to carry out that work.

Accomplishments/Achievements

This section relates the various activities you have been involved in to the job market. These experiences may include previous jobs, extracurricular activities at school, internships, and part-time summer work.

Experience

Your work history should be listed in abbreviated form and may include position title, employer name, and employment dates.

Education

Because this type of resume is directed toward a specific job target and an individual's related experience, the education section is not prominently located at the top of the resume as is done on the chronological resume.

THE BROADCAST LETTER

The broadcast letter is used by some job seekers in place of a resume and cover letter. (See Exhibit 2.5.) The purpose of this type of document is to make a number of potential employers aware of the availability and expertise of the job seeker. Because the broadcast letter is mass-mailed (500–600 employers), the amount of work required may not be worth the return for many people. If you choose to mail out a broadcast letter, you can expect to receive a response from 2–5 percent, at best, of the organizations that receive your letter.

Exhibit 2.5

Broadcast Letter

CHRISTOPHER JAMES

4324 Travis Road
Houston, TX 77504
(713) 555-3632

June 6, 1998

Mr. Stephen Lyons
Human Resources Director
Rawlings Oil Corporation
5465 Lincoln Road
Houston, TX 77525

Dear Mr. Lyons,

I am writing to you because your corporation may be in need of an accountant with a specialization in internal auditing. With my master's degree from the University of Texas–Austin in business management and my four years of increasing experience in a variety of settings, I have had the opportunity to work with a

continued

---

continued

cross-section of clients with a range of needs. I am able to adapt to different environments and put my skills and abilities to immediate use. Some highlights of my experience that might interest you include:

- Interned with the Internal Revenue Service my senior year in undergraduate school as a field agent for three different branches: Collections, Examination, and Criminal Investigation.

- Worked for three years for a major corporation in Dallas, Texas, in the finance department as assistant internal auditor, checking at the company's request for mismanagement, waste, or fraud. As the result of my investigation, new management policies were adopted.

- Supervised bachelor's level accounting majors in work-study positions at the aforementioned company.

I received my B.A. in accounting in 1995 and my M.B.A. with a concentration in accounting in 1996, both from the University of Texas–Austin.
It would be a pleasure to review my qualifications with you in a personal interview at some mutually convenient time. I will call your office at the end of next week to make arrangements. I look forward to discussing with you career opportunities with Rawlings Oil Corporation.

Sincerely,

Christopher James, CPA, CIA

This type of document is most often used by individuals who have an extensive and quantifiable work history. College students often do not have the credentials and work experience to support using a broadcast letter, and most will find it difficult to effectively quantify a slim work history.

A broadcast letter is generally four paragraphs (one page) long. The first paragraph should immediately gain the attention of the reader and state some unusual accomplishment or skill that would be of benefit to the organization. It also states the reason for the letter. Details of the sender's work history are revealed in the third paragraph. These can appear in paragraph form or as a bulleted list. Education and other qualifications or credentials are then described. Finally, the job seeker indicates what he or she will do to follow up on the letter, which usually is a follow-up call 1 to 2 weeks after the letter is sent.

RESUME PRODUCTION AND OTHER TIPS

If you have the option and convenience of using a laser printer, you may want to initially produce a limited number of copies in case you want or need to make changes on your resume.

Resume paper color should be carefully chosen. You should consider the types of employers who will receive your resume and the types of positions for which you are applying. Use white or ivory paper for traditional or conservative employers, or for higher-level positions.

Black ink on sharply white paper can be harsh on the reader's eyes. Think about an ivory or cream paper that will provide less contrast and be easier to read. Pink, green, and blue tints should generally be avoided.

Many resume writers buy packages of matching envelopes and cover sheet stationery that, although not absolutely necessary, does convey a professional impression.

If you'll be producing many cover letters at home, be sure you have high-quality printing equipment, whether it be computerized or standard typewriter equipment. Learn standard envelope formats for business and retain a copy of every cover letter you send out. You can use it to take notes of any telephone conversations that may occur.

If attending a job fair, women generally can fold their resume in thirds lengthwise and find it fits into a clutch bag or envelope-style purse. Both men and women will have no trouble if they carry a briefcase. For men without a briefcase, carry the resume in a nicely covered legal-size pad holder or fold it in half lengthwise and place it inside your suitcoat pocket, taking care it doesn't "float" outside your collar.

THE COVER LETTER

The cover letter provides you with the opportunity to tailor your resume by telling the prospective employer how you can be a benefit to the organization. It will allow you to highlight aspects of your background that are not already discussed in your resume and that might be especially relevant to the organization you are contacting or to the position you are seeking. Every resume should have a cover letter enclosed when you send it out. Unlike the resume, which may be mass-produced, a cover letter is most effective when it is individually typed and focused on the particular requirements of the organization in question.

A good cover letter should supplement the resume and motivate the reader to review the resume. The format shown in Exhibit 2.6 is only a suggestion to help you decide what information to include in writing a cover letter.

Begin the cover letter with your street address 12 lines down from the top. Leave three to five lines between the date and the name of the person to whom you are addressing the cover letter. Make sure you leave one blank line between the salutation and the body of the letter and between each paragraph.

After typing "Sincerely," leave four blank lines and type your name. This should leave plenty of room for your signature. A sample cover letter is shown in Exhibit 2.7.

Exhibit 2.6

Cover Letter Format

Your Street Address
Your Town, State, Zip
Phone Number
Date
Name
Title
Organization
Address

Dear _____ :

First Paragraph. In this paragraph, state the reason for the letter, name the specific position or type of work you are applying for, and indicate from which resource (career development office, newspaper, contact, employment service) you learned of the opening. The first paragraph can also be used to inquire about future openings.

Second Paragraph. Indicate why you are interested in the position, the company, its products or services, and what you can do for the employer. If you are a recent graduate, explain how your academic background makes you a qualified candidate. Try not to repeat the same information found in the resume.

continued

continued

Third Paragraph. Refer the reader to the enclosed resume for more detailed information.

Fourth Paragraph. In this paragraph, say what you will do to follow up on your letter. For example, state that you will call by a certain date to set up an interview or to find out if the company will be recruiting in your area. Finish by indicating your willingness to answer any questions they may have. Be sure you have provided your phone number.

Sincerely,

Type your name

Enclosure

The following are guidelines that will help you write good cover letters:

1. Be sure to type your letter; ensure there are no misspellings.

2. Avoid unusual typefaces, such as script.

3. Address the letter to an individual, using the person's name and title. To obtain this information, call the company. If answering a blind newspaper advertisement, address the letter "To Whom It May Concern" or omit the salutation.

4. Be sure your cover letter directly indicates the position you are applying for and tells why you are qualified to fill it.

5. Send the original letter, not a photocopy, with your resume. Keep a copy for your records.

6. Make your cover letter no more than one page.

7. Include a phone number where you can be reached.

8. Avoid trite language and have someone read it over to react to its tone, content, and mechanics.

9. For your own information, record the date you send out each letter and resume.

Exhibit 2.7

Sample Cover Letter

JANE DUSTIN

229 Kelton Street #4
Brighton, MA 02135
(617) 555-3333

May 10 , 1998

Diane Irving
Director of Personnel
Sterling Museum
65 The Fenway
Boston, MA 02115

Dear Ms. Irving:

In June of 1998 I will graduate from Boston University with a bachelor's degree in business management with a specialization in accounting. I read of your opening for an assistant management accountant in *The Globe* on Sunday, May 9, 1998, and I am very interested in the possibilities it offers. I am writing to explore the opportunity for employment with your museum.

The ad indicated that you are looking for creative team players with good communication skills as well as quantitative skills and management accounting experience. I believe I possess those qualities. While interning at the Boston Museum of Fine Arts I learned the ins and outs of the financial workings of a major museum, including the importance of teamwork.

In addition to the various accounting courses in my academic program, I studied art history (my first love), museum studies, and computer science, including the use of spreadsheets and databases. These courses helped me become familiar with the inner workings of museums and their collections and familiarize myself with a variety of computer accounting systems. I believe that this experience, coupled with my enthusiasm for working in an art museum environment, will help me to represent Sterling Museum in a professional and competent manner.

continued

continued

As you will see in my enclosed resume, I worked at the Museum of Fine Arts for a total of three years, both in the finance office and under the direction of the collections manager for eighteenth-century European art. These placements provided me with experience tracking both artwork and finances and allowed me to see how both offices function cooperatively.

I would like to meet with you to discuss how my education and experience would be consistent with your needs. I will contact your office next week to discuss the possibility of an interview. In the meantime, if you have any questions or require additional information, please contact me by phone at (617) 555-3333 or via email at Jdust@aol.com.

Sincerely,

Jane Dustin
Enclosure

CHAPTER THREE

RESEARCHING CAREERS

· ·

One common question a career counselor encounters is "What can I do with my degree?" Accounting majors have narrowed their interests more than most liberal arts graduates, but still all their choices are not clearly defined. Accounting majors might know the type of accounting work they want to do—income tax returns or worker's comp, public or private, government or corporate—but they could be unsure of the various job settings in which work is available and satisfying. The field might seem so open that the job search is at first daunting—almost every type of service, industry, or institution requires the services of a professional accountant. Would you fit in more comfortably at a large corporation, a small private business, the IRS, a hospital, an educational institution, or any other number of settings? The choices really are limitless.

· ·

WHAT DO THEY CALL THE JOB YOU WANT?

There is every reason to be unaware. One reason for confusion is perhaps a mistaken assumption that a college education provides job training. In most cases, it does not. Of course, applied fields such as engineering, management, or education provide specific skills for the workplace, whereas most liberal arts degrees simply provide an education. A liberal arts education exposes you to numerous fields of study and teaches you quantitative reasoning, critical thinking, writing, and speaking, all of which can be successfully applied to a number of different job fields. But it still remains up to you to choose a job field and to learn how to articulate the benefits of your education in a way the employer will appreciate.

As indicated in Chapter 1 on self-assessment, your first task is to understand and value what parts of that education you enjoyed and were good at and would continue to enjoy in your life's work. Did your writing courses encourage you in your ability to express yourself in writing? Did you enjoy the research process and did you find your work was well received? Did you enjoy any of your required quantitative subjects like algebra or calculus?

The answers to questions such as these provide clues to skills and interests you bring to the employment market over and above the credential of your degree. In fact, it is not an overstatement to suggest that most employers who demand a college degree immediately look beyond that degree to you as a person and your own individual expression of what you like to do and think you can do for them, regardless of your major.

COLLECTING JOB TITLES

The world of employment is a big place, and even seasoned veterans of the job hunt can be surprised about what jobs are to be found in what organizations. You need to become a bit of an explorer and adventurer and be willing to try a variety of techniques to begin a list of possible occupations that might use your talents and education. Once you have a list of possibilities that you are interested in and qualified for, you can move on to find out what kinds of organizations have these job titles.

Not every employer seeking to hire someone with an accounting degree may be equally desirable to you. Some employment environments may be more attractive to you than others. An accountant wanting to work in auditing could do so in a large corporation, a small firm within a corporation, a private concern, the government, a financial institution, or even a hospital. Each of these environments presents a different corporate culture with associated norms in the pace of work, the subject matter of interest, and the backgrounds of its employees. Although the job titles may be the same, not all locations may present the same fit for you.

If you majored in accounting and enjoyed the exacting, detailed work you did as part of your studies and if you have developed some strong investigative skills, you might naturally think about forensic accounting. But accounting majors with these same skills and interests might go on to teach others their skills, or work as actuaries or statisticians. Each of these job titles can also be found in a number of different settings.

....

Take training, for example. Trainers write policy and procedural manuals and actively teach to assist all levels of employees in mastering various tasks and work-related systems. Trainers exist in all large corporations, banks, consumer goods manufacturers, medical diagnostic equipment firms, sales organizations, and any organization that has processes or materials that need to be presented to and learned by the staff.

In reading job descriptions or want ads for any of these positions, you would find your four-year degree a "must." However, the academic major might be less important than your own individual skills in critical thinking, analysis, report writing, public presentations, and interpersonal communication. Even more important than thinking or knowing you have certain skills is your ability to express those skills concretely and the examples you use to illustrate them to an employer.

The best beginning to a job search is to create a list of job titles you might want to pursue, learn more about the nature of the jobs behind those titles, and then discover what kinds of employers hire for those positions. In the following section, we'll teach you how to build a job title directory to use in your job search.

Developing a Job Title Directory That Works for You

A job title directory is simply a complete list of all the job titles you are interested in, are intrigued by, or think you are qualified for. Combining the understanding gained through self-assessment with your own individual interests and the skills and talents you've acquired with your degree, you'll soon start to read and recognize a number of occupational titles that seem right for you. There are several resources you can use to develop your list, including computer searches, books, and want ads.

Computerized Interest Inventories. One way to begin your search is to identify a number of jobs that call for your degree and the particular skills and interests you identified as part of the self-assessment process. There are excellent interactive computer career guidance programs on the market to help you produce such selected lists of possible job titles. Most of these are available at high schools and colleges and at some larger town and city libraries. Two of the industry leaders are SIGI and DISCOVER. Both allow you to enter interests, values, educational background, and other information to produce lists of possible occupations and industries. Each of the resources listed here will produce different job title lists. Some job titles will appear again and again, while others will be unique to a particular source. Investigate them all!

Reference Books. Books on the market that may be available through your local library, bookstore, or career counseling office also suggest various occupations related to a number of majors. The following are only two of the many good books on the market: *Occupational Outlook Handbook* and *Occupational Projections and Training Data,* both put out annually by the U.S. Department of Labor, Bureau of Labor Statistics. The *OOH* describes hundreds of job titles under several broad categories such as Executive, Administrative, and Managerial Occupations and also identifies those jobs by their *Dictionary of Occupational Titles* (DOT) code. (See following discussion.)

· ·

For accounting majors, more than 40 job titles are listed. Some are familiar ones such as public accountant or auditor, and others are interestingly different, such as forensic accountant or budget analyst.

The *Occupational Thesaurus* is another good resource, listing job title possibilities under general categories. So, if you see internal job auditor as a job title in the book *What Can I Do with a Major in . . . ?,* you can then go to the *Occupational Thesaurus,* which lists scores of jobs under that title. This source adds some depth by suggesting a number of different occupations within that field.

· ·

Each job title deserves your consideration. Like the layers of an onion, the search for job titles can go on and on! As you spend time doing this activity, you are actually learning more about the value of your degree. What's important in your search at this point is not to become critical or selective, but rather to develop as long a list of possibilities as you can. Every source used will help you add new and potentially exciting jobs to your growing list.

Want Ads. It has been well publicized that newspaper want ads represent only about 10–15 percent of the current job market. Nevertheless, the Sunday want ads can be a great help to you in your search. Although they may not be the best place to look for a job, they can teach the job seeker much about the job market and provide a good education in job descriptions, duties and responsibilities, active industries, and some indication of the volume of job traffic. For our purposes, they are a good source for job titles to add to your list.

Read the Sunday want ads in a major market newspaper for several Sundays in a row. Circle and cut out any and all ads that interest you and seem to call for something close to your education and experience. Remember, because want ads are written for what an organization *hopes* to find, you don't have to meet absolutely every criterion. However, if certain requirements are stated as absolute minimums and you cannot meet them, it's best not to waste your time.

A recent examination of *The Boston Sunday Globe* reveals the following possible occupations for a liberal arts major with some computer skills and limited prior work experience. (This is only a partial list of what was available.)

- Admissions representative
- Salesperson
- Compliance director
- Assistant principal gifts writer
- Public relations officer
- Technical writer
- Personnel trainee
- GED examiner
- Direct mail researcher
- Associate publicist

After performing this exercise for a few Sundays, you'll find you have collected a new library of job titles.

The Sunday want ad exercise is important because these jobs are out in the marketplace. They truly exist, and people with your qualifications are being sought to apply. What's more, many of these advertisements describe the duties and responsibilities of the job advertised and give you a beginning sense of the challenges and opportunities such a position presents. Some will indicate salary, and that will be helpful as well. This information will better define the jobs for you and provide some good material for possible interviews in that field.

Exploring Job Descriptions

Once you've arrived at a solid list of possible job titles that interest you and for which you believe you are somewhat qualified, it's a good idea to do some research on each of these jobs. The preeminent source for such job information is the *Dictionary of Occupational Titles,* or DOT. This directory lists every conceivable job and provides excellent up-to-date information on duties and responsibilities, interactions with associates, and day-to-day assignments and tasks. These descriptions provide a thorough job analysis, but they do not consider the possible employers or the environments in which this job may be performed. So, although a position as public relations officer may be well defined in terms of duties and responsibilities, it does not explain the differences in doing public relations work in a college or a hospital or a factory or a bank. You will need to look somewhere else for work settings.

Learning More About Possible Work Settings

After reading some job descriptions, you may choose to edit and revise your list of job titles once again, discarding those you feel are not suitable and keeping those that continue to hold your interest. Or you may wish to keep your list intact and see where these jobs may be located. For example, if you are interested in public relations and you appear to have those skills and the requisite education, you'll want to know what organizations do public relations. How can you find that out? How much income does someone in public relations make a year and what is the employment potential for the field of public relations?

To answer these and many other good questions about your list of job titles, we will direct you to any of the following resources: *Careers Encyclopedia, Career Information Center, College to Career: The Guide to Job Opportunities,* and the *Occupational Outlook Handbook.* Each of these books, in a different way, will help to put the job titles you have selected into an employer context. *VGM'S Handbook for Business and Management Careers* shows detailed career descriptions for over fifty fields. Entries include complete information on duties and responsibilities for individual careers and detailed entry-level requirements. There is information on working conditions and promotional opportunities as well. Salary ranges and career outlook projections are also provided. Perhaps the most extensive discussion is found in the *Occupational Outlook Handbook,* which gives a thorough presentation of the nature of the work, the working conditions, employment statistics, training, other qualifications, and advancement possibilities as well as job outlook and earnings. Related occupations are also detailed, and a select bibliography is provided to help you find additional information.

Continuing with our public relations example, your search through these reference materials would teach you that the public relations jobs you find attractive are available in larger hospitals, financial institutions, most corporations (both consumer goods and industrial goods), media organizations, and colleges and universities.

Networking to Get the Complete Story

You now have not only a list of job titles but also, for each of these job titles, a description of the work involved and a general list of possible employment settings in which to work. You'll want to do some reading and keep talking to friends, colleagues, teachers, and others about the possibilities. Don't neglect to ask if the career office at your college maintains some kind of alumni network. Often such alumni networks will connect you with another graduate from the college who is working in the job title or industry you are seeking information about. These career networkers offer what assistance they can. For some, it is a full day "shadowing" the alumnus as he or she goes about the job. Others offer partial day visits, tours, informational interviews, resume reviews, job postings, or, if distance prevents a visit, telephone interviews. As fellow graduates, they'll be frank and informative about their own jobs and prospects in their field.

Take them up on their offer and continue to learn all you can about your own personal list of job titles, descriptions, and employment settings. You'll probably continue to edit and refine this list as you learn more about the realities of the job, the possible salary, advancement opportunities, and supply and demand statistics.

In the next section, we'll describe how to find the specific organizations that represent these industries and employers, so that you can begin to make contact.

WHERE ARE THESE JOBS, ANYWAY?

Having a list of job titles that you've designed around your own career interests and skills is an excellent beginning. It means you've really thought about who you are and what you are presenting to the employment market. It has caused you to think seriously about the most appealing environments to work in, and you have identified some employer types that represent these environments.

The research and the thinking that you've done this far will be used again and again. It will be helpful in writing your resume and cover letters, in talking about yourself on the telephone to prospective employers, and in answering interview questions.

Now is a good time to begin to narrow the field of job titles and employment sites down to some specific employers to initiate the employment contact.

Finding Out Which Employers Hire People Like You

This section will provide tips, techniques, and specific resources for developing an actual list of specific employers that can be used to make contacts. It is only an outline that you must be prepared to tailor to your own particular needs and according to what you bring to the job search. Once again, it is important to stress the need to communicate with others along the way exactly what you're looking for and what your goals are for the research you're doing. Librarians, employers, career counselors, friends, friends of friends, business contacts, and bookstore staff will all have helpful information on geographically specific and new resources to aid you in locating employers who'll hire you.

Identifying Information Resources

Your interview wardrobe and your new resume may have put a dent in your wallet, but the resources you'll need to pursue your job search are available for free (although you might choose to copy materials on a machine instead of taking notes by hand). The categories of information detailed here are not hard to find and are yours for the browsing.

Numerous resources described in this section will help you identify actual employers. Use all of them or any others that you identify as available in your geographic area. As you become experienced in this process, you'll quickly figure out which information sources are helpful and which are not. If you live in a rural area, a well-planned day trip to a major city that includes a college career office, a large college or city library, state and federal employment centers, a chamber of commerce office, and a well-stocked bookstore can produce valuable results.

There are many excellent resources available to help you identify actual job sites. They are categorized into employer directories (usually indexed by product lines and geographic location), geographically based directories (designed to highlight particular cities, regions, or states), career-specific directories (e.g., *Sports Market Place,* which lists tens of thousands of firms involved with sports), periodicals and newspapers, targeted job posting publications, and videos. This is by no means meant to be a complete list of resources, but rather a starting point for identifying useful resources.

Working from the more general references to highly specific resources, we will provide a basic list to help you begin your search. Many of these you'll find easily available. In some cases, reference librarians and others will suggest even better materials for your particular situation. Start to create your own customized bibliography of job search references. Use copying services to save time and to allow you to carry away information about organization mission, location, company officers, phone numbers, and addresses.

Employer Directories. There are many employer directories available to give you the kind of information you need for your job search. Some of our favorites are listed here, but be sure to ask the professionals you are working with to make additional suggestions.

- *America's Corporate Families* identifies many major U.S. ultimate parent companies and displays corporate family linkage of subsidiaries and divisions. Businesses can be identified by their industrial code.

- *Million Dollar Directory: America's Leading Public and Private Companies* lists about 160,000 companies.

- *Moody's* various manuals are intended as guides for investors, so they contain a history of each company. Each manual contains a classification of companies by industries and products.

- *Standard and Poor's Register of Corporations* contains listings for 45,000 businesses, some of which are not listed in the *Million Dollar Directory.*

- *Job Seekers Guide to Private and Public Companies* profiles 15,000 employers in four volumes, each covering a different geographic region. Company entries include contact information, business descriptions, and application procedures.

- *The Career Guide: Dun's Employment Opportunities Directory* lists more than 5,000 large organizations, including hospitals and local governments. Profiles include an overview and history of the employer as well as opportunities, benefits, and contact names. It contains geographic and industrial indexes and indexes by discipline or internship availability. This guide also includes a state-by-state list of professional personnel consultants and their specialties.

- *Professional's Job Finder/Government Job Finder/Non-Profits Job Finder* are specific directories of job services, salary surveys, and periodical listings in which advertisements for jobs in the professional, government, or not-for-profit sector are found.

- *Opportunities in Nonprofit Organizations* is a VGM career series edition that opens up the world of not-for-profit by helping you match your interest profile to the aims and objectives of scores of nonprofit employers in business, education, health and medicine, social welfare, science and technology, and many others. There is also a special section on fundraising and development career paths.

❑ *The 100 Best Companies to Sell For* lists companies by industry and provides contact information and describes benefits and corporate culture.

❑ *The 100 Best Companies to Work for in America* rates organizations on several factors including opportunities, job security, and pay.

❑ *Companies That Care* lists organizations that the authors believe are family-friendly. One index organizes information by state.

❑ *Infotrac* CD-ROM *Business Index* covers business journals and magazines as well as news magazines and can provide information on public and private companies.

❑ *ABI/INFORM on Disc* (CD-ROM) indexes articles in over 800 journals.

Geographically Based Directories. The Job Bank series published by Bob Adams, Inc. contains detailed entries on each area's major employers, including business activity, address, phone number, and hiring contact name. Many listings specify educational backgrounds being sought in potential employees. Each volume contains a solid discussion of each city's or state's major employment sectors. Organizations are also indexed by industry. Job Bank volumes are available for the following places: Atlanta, Boston, Chicago, Denver, Dallas-Ft. Worth, Florida, Houston, Ohio, St. Louis, San Francisco, Seattle, Los Angeles, New York, Detroit, Philadelphia, Minneapolis, the Northwest, and Washington, D.C.

National Job Bank lists employers in every state, along with contact names and commonly hired job categories. Included are many small companies often overlooked by other directories. Companies are also indexed by industry. This publication provides information on educational backgrounds sought and lists company benefits.

Career-Specific Directories. VGM publishes a number of excellent series detailing careers for college graduates. In the *Professional Career Series* are guides to careers in the following fields, among others:

❑ Advertising

❑ Communications

❑ Business

❑ Computers

❑ Health Care

❑ High Tech

Each provides an excellent discussion of the industry, educational requirements for jobs, salary ranges, duties, and projected outlooks for the field.

Another VGM series, *Opportunities In . . .,* has an equally wide range of
titles relating to specific majors, such as the following:

- ❑ *Opportunities in Banking*

- ❑ *Opportunities in Insurance*

- ❑ *Opportunities in Sports and Athletics*

- ❑ *Opportunities in Journalism*

- ❑ *Opportunities in Marketing*

- ❑ *Opportunities in Television and Radio*

Sports Market Place (Sportsguide) lists organizations by sport. It also describes
trade/professional associations, college athletic organizations, multi-sport
publications, media contacts, corporate sports sponsors, promotion/event/ath-
letic management services, and trade shows.

Periodicals and Newspapers. Several sources are available to help you locate
which journals or magazines carry job advertisements in your field. Other
resources help you identify opportunities in other parts of the country.

- ❑ *Where the Jobs Are: A Comprehensive Directory of 1,200 Journals Listing
  Career Opportunities* links specific occupational titles to corresponding
  periodicals that carry job listings for your field.

- ❑ *Social & Behavioral Sciences Jobs Handbook* contains a periodicals
  matrix organized by academic discipline and highlights periodicals
  containing job listings.

- ❑ *National Business Employment Weekly* compiles want ads from four
  regional editions of the *Wall Street Journal.* Most are business and
  management positions.

- ❑ *National Ad Search* reprints ads from seventy-five metropolitan
  newspapers across the country. Although the focus is on management
  positions, technical and professional postings are also included.
  Caution: Watch deadline dates carefully on listings, because deadlines
  may have already passed by the time the ad is printed.

- ❑ *The Federal Jobs Digest* and *Federal Career Opportunities* list
  government positions.

❑ *World Chamber of Commerce Directory* lists addresses for chambers worldwide, state boards of tourism, convention and visitors' bureaus, and economic development organizations.

This list is certainly not exhaustive; use it to begin your job search work.

Targeted Job Posting Publications. Although the resources that follow are national in scope, they are either targeted to one medium of contact (telephone), focused on specific types of jobs, or are less comprehensive than the sources previously listed.

❑ *Job Hotlines USA* pinpoints over 1,000 hard-to-find telephone numbers for companies and government agencies that use prerecorded job messages and listings. Very few of the telephone numbers listed are toll-free, and sometimes recordings are long, so callers beware!

❑ *The Job Hunter* is a national biweekly newspaper listing business, arts, media, government, human services, health, community-related, and student services job openings.

❑ *Current Jobs for Graduates* is a national employment listing for liberal arts professions, including editorial positions, management opportunities, museum work, teaching, and nonprofit work.

❑ *Environmental Opportunities* serves environmental job interests nationwide by listing administrative, marketing, and human resources positions along with education-related jobs and positions directly related to a degree in an environmental field.

❑ *Y National Vacancy List* shows YMCA professional vacancies, including development, administration, programming, membership, and recreation postings.

❑ *ARTSearch* is a national employment service bulletin for the arts, including administration, managerial, marketing, and financial management jobs.

❑ *Community Jobs* is an employment newspaper for the nonprofit sector that provides a variety of listings, including project manager, canvas director, government relations specialist, community organizer, and program instructor.

❑ *College Placement Council Annual: A Guide to Employment Opportunities for College Graduates* is an annual guide containing solid job-hunting information and, more importantly, displaying ads from large corporations actively seeking recent college graduates in all majors. Company profiles provide brief descriptions and available employment opportunities. Contact names and addresses are given. Profiles are indexed by organization name, geographic location, and occupation.

Videos. You may be one of the many job seekers who like to get information via a medium other than paper. Many career libraries, public libraries, and career centers in libraries carry an assortment of videos that will help you learn new techniques and get information helpful in the job search. A small sampling of the multitude of videos now available includes the following:

❑ *The Skills Search* (20 min.) discusses three types of skills important in the workplace, how to present the skills in an interview, and how to respond to problem questions.

❑ *Effective Answers to Interview Questions* (35 min.) presents two real-life job seekers and shows how they realized the true meaning of interview questions and formulated positive answers.

❑ *Employers Expectations* (33 min.) covers three areas that are important to all employers: appearance, dependability, and skills.

❑ *The Tough New Labor Market of the 1990s* (30 min.) presents labor market facts as well as suggestions on what job seekers should do to gain employment in this market.

❑ *Dialing for Jobs: Using the Phone in the Job Search* (30 min.) describes how to use the phone effectively to gain information and arrange interviews by following two new graduates as they learn and apply techniques.

Locating Information Resources

An essay by John Case that appeared in the *Boston Globe* (August 25, 1993) alerts both new and seasoned job seekers that the job market is changing, and the old guarantees of lifelong employment no longer hold true. Some of our major corporations, which were once seen as the most prestigious of employment destinations, are now laying off thousands of employees. Middle management is especially hard hit in downsizing situations. On the other side of the coin, smaller, more entrepreneurial firms are adding employees and realizing enormous profit margins. The geography of the new job market is unfamiliar, and the terrain is much harder to map. New and smaller firms can mean different kinds of jobs and new job titles. The successful job seeker will keep an open mind about where he or she might find employment and what that employment might be called.

In order to become familiar with this new terrain, you will need to undertake some research, which can be done at any of the following locations:

- Public libraries

- Business organizations

- Employment agencies

- Bookstores

- Career libraries

Each one of these places offers a collection of resources that will help you get the information you need.

As you meet and talk with service professionals at all these sites, be sure to let them know what you're doing. Inform them of your job search, what you've already accomplished, and what you're looking for. The more people who know you're job seeking, the greater the possibility that someone will have information or know someone who can help you along your way.

Public Libraries. Large city libraries, college and university libraries, and even well-supported town library collections contain a variety of resources to help you conduct a job search. It is not uncommon for libraries to have separate "vocational choices" sections with books, tapes, and associated materials relating to job search and selection. Some are now even making resume creation software available for use by patrons.

Some of the publications we name throughout this book are expensive reference items that are rarely purchased by individuals. In addition, libraries carry a wide range of newspapers and telephone yellow pages as well as the usual array of books. If resources are not immediately available, many libraries have loan arrangements with other facilities and can make information available to you relatively quickly.

Take advantage of not only the reference collections, but also the skilled and informed staff. Let them know exactly what you are looking for, and they'll have their own suggestions. You'll be visiting the library frequently, and the reference staff will soon come to know who you are and what you're working on. They'll be part of your job search network!

Business Organizations. Chambers of Commerce, Offices of New Business Development, Councils on Business and Industry, Small Business Administration (SBA) offices, and professional associations can all provide geographically specific lists of companies and organizations that have hiring needs. They also have an array of other available materials, including visitors' guides and regional fact books that provide additional employment information.

These agencies serve to promote local and regional businesses and ensure their survival and success. Although these business organizations do not advertise job openings or seek employees for their members, they may be very aware of staffing needs among their member firms. In your visits to each of these locations, spend some time with the personnel getting to know who they are and what they do. Let them know of your job search and your intentions regarding employment. You may be surprised and delighted at the information they may provide.

Employment Agencies. Employment agencies (including state and federal employment offices), professional "head hunters" or executive search firms, and some private career counselors can provide direct leads to job openings. Don't overlook these resources. If you are mounting a complete job search program and want to ensure that you are covering the potential market for employers, consider the employment agencies in your territory. Some of these organizations work contractually with several specific firms and may have access that is unavailable to you. Others may be particularly well-informed about supply and demand in particular industries or geographic locations.

In the case of professional (commercial) employment agencies, which include those executive recruitment firms labeled "head hunters," you should be cautious about entering into any binding contractual agreement. Before doing so, be sure to get the information you need to decide whether their services can be of use to you. Questions to ask include the following: Who pays the fee when employment is obtained? Are there any other fees or costs associated with this service? What is their placement rate? Can you see a list of previous clients and can you talk to any for references? Do they typically work with entry-level job seekers? Do they tend to focus on particular kinds of employment or industries?

A few cautions are in order, however, when you work with professional agencies. Remember, the professional employment agency is, in most cases, paid by the hiring organization. Naturally, their interest and attention is largely directed to the employer, not to the candidate. Of course, they want to provide good candidates to guarantee future contracts, but they are less interested in the job seeker than the employer.

For teacher candidates, there are a number of good placement firms that charge the prospective teacher, not the employer. This situation has evolved over time as a result of supply and demand and financial structuring of most school systems, which cannot spend money on recruiting teachers. Usually these firms charge a nonrefundable administrative fee and, upon successful placement, require a fee based on percentage of salary, which may range from 10–20 percent of annual compensation. Often, this can be repaid over a number of months. Check your contract carefully.

State and federal employment offices are no-fee services that maintain extensive "job boards" and can provide detailed specifications for each job advertised and help with application forms. Because government employment application forms are detailed, keep a master copy along with copies of all additional documentation (resumes, educational transcripts, military discharge papers, proof of citizenship, etc.). Successive applications may require separate filings. Visit these offices as frequently as you can, because most deal with applicants on a "walk-in" basis and will not telephone prospective candidates or maintain files of job seekers. Check your telephone book for the address of the nearest state and federal offices.

One type of employment service that causes much confusion among job seekers is the outplacement firm. Their advertisements tend to suggest they will put you in touch with the "hidden job market." They use advertising phrases such as "We'll work with you until you get that job," or "Maximize your earnings and career opportunities." In fact, if you read the fine print on these ads, you will notice these firms must state they are "Not an employment agency." These firms are, in fact, corporate and private outplacement counseling agencies whose work involves resume editing, counseling to provide leads for jobs, interview skills training, and all the other aspects of hiring preparation. They do this for a fee, sometimes in the thousands of dollars range, which is paid by you, the client. Some of these firms have good reputations and provide excellent materials and techniques. Most, however, provide a service you as a college student or graduate can receive free from your alma mater or through a reciprocity agreement between your college and a college or university located closer to your current address.

Bookstores. Any well-stocked bookstore will carry some job search books that are worth buying. Some major stores will even have an extensive section devoted to materials, including excellent videos, related to the job search process. Several possibilities are listed in following sections. You will also find copies of local newspapers and business magazines. The one advantage that is provided by resources purchased at a bookstore is that you can read and work with the information in the comfort of your own home and do not have to conform to the hours of operation of a library, which can present real difficulties if you are working full time as you seek employment. A few minutes spent browsing in a bookstore might be a beneficial break from your job search activities and turn up valuable resources.

Career Libraries. Career libraries, which are found in career centers at colleges and universities and sometimes within large public libraries, contain a unique blend of the job search resources housed in other settings. In addition, career libraries often purchase a number of job listing publications, each of which targets a specific industry or type of job. You may find job listings specifically for entry-level positions for accounting majors. Ask about job posting newsletters or newspapers specifically focused on careers in the area that most interests you. Each center will be unique, but you are certain to discover some good sources of jobs.

Most college career libraries now hold growing collections of video material on specific industries and on aspects of your job search process, including dress and appearance, how to manage the luncheon or dinner interview, how to be effective at a job fair, and many other specific titles. Some larger corporations produce handsome video materials detailing the variety of career paths and opportunities available in their organizations.

Some career libraries also house computer-based career planning and information systems. These interactive computer programs help you to clarify your values and interests and will combine that with your education to provide possible job titles and industry locations. Some even contain extensive lists of graduate school programs.

One specific kind of service a career library will be able to direct you to is computerized job search services. These services, of which there are many, are run by private companies, individual colleges, or consortiums of colleges. They attempt to match qualified job candidates with potential employers. The candidate submits a resume (or an application) to the service. This information (which can be categorized into hundreds of separate "fields" of data) is entered into a computer database. Your information is then compared with the information from employers about what they desire in a prospective employee. If there is a "match" between what they want and what you have indicated you can offer, the job search service or the employer will contact you directly to continue the process.

Computerized job search services can complement an otherwise complete job search program. They are not, however, a substitute for the kinds of activities described in this book. They are essentially passive operations that are random in nature. If you have not listed skills, abilities, traits, experiences, or education exactly as an employer has listed its needs, there is simply no match.

Consult with the staff members at the career libraries you use. These professionals have been specifically trained to meet the unique needs you present. Often you can just drop in and receive help with general questions, or you may want to set up an appointment to speak one-on-one with a career counselor to gain special assistance.

Every career library is different in size and content, but each can provide valuable information for the job search. Some may even provide some limited counseling. If you have not visited the career library at your college or alma mater, call and ask if these collections are still available for your use. Be sure to ask about other services that you can use as well.

If you are not near your own college as you work on your job search, call the career office and inquire about reciprocal agreements with other colleges that are closer to where you live. Very often, your own alma mater can arrange for you to use a limited menu of services at another school. This typically would include access to a career library and job posting information and might include limited counseling.

CHAPTER FOUR

NETWORKING

*N*etworking is the process of deliberately establishing relationships to get career-related information or to alert potential employers that you are available for work. Networking is critically important to today's job seeker for two reasons: it will help you get the information you need, and it can help you find out about *all* of the available jobs.

Getting the Information You Need

Networkers will review your resume and give you candid feedback on its effectiveness. They will talk about the job you are looking for and give you a candid appraisal of how they see your strengths and weaknesses. If they have a good sense of the industry or the employment sector for that job, you'll get their feelings on future trends in the industry as well. Some networkers will be very candid about salaries, job hunting techniques, and suggestions for your job search strategy. Many have been known to place calls right from the interview desk to friends and associates that might be interested in you. Each networker will make his or her own contribution, and each will be valuable.

Because organizations must evolve to adapt to current global market needs, the information provided by decision-makers within various organizations will be critical to your success as a new job market entrant. For example, you might learn about the concept of virtual organizations from a networker. Virtual organizations are those that are temporarily established to take advantage of fast-changing opportunities and then dissolved. This concept is being discussed and implemented by chief executive officers of many organizations, including Corning, Apple, and Digital. Networking can help you find out about this and other trends currently affecting the industries under your consideration.

Finding Out About All of the Available Jobs

Secondly, not every job that is available at this very moment is advertised for potential applicants to see. This is called the *hidden job market*. Only 15 to 20 percent of all jobs are formally advertised, which means that 80 to 85 percent of available jobs do not appear in published channels. Networking will help you become more knowledgeable about all the employment opportunities available during your job search period.

Although someone you might talk to today doesn't know of any openings within his or her organization, tomorrow or next week or next month an opening may occur. If you've taken the time to show an interest in and knowledge of their organization, if you've shown the company representative how you can help achieve organizational goals and that you can fit into the organization, you'll be one of the first candidates considered for the position.

Networking: A Proactive Approach

Networking is a proactive rather than a reactive approach. You, as a job seeker, are expected to initiate a certain level of activity on your own behalf; you cannot afford to simply respond to jobs listed in the newspaper. Being proactive means building a network of contacts that includes informed and interested decision-makers who will provide you with up-to-date knowledge of the current job market and increase your chances of finding out about employment opportunities appropriate for your interests, experience, and level of education.

An old axiom of networking says, "You are only two phone calls away from the information you need." In other words, by talking to enough people, you will quickly come across someone who can offer you help. Start with your professors. Each of them probably has a wide circle of contacts. In their work and travel they might have met someone who can help you or direct you to someone who can.

Control and the Networking Process

In deliberately establishing relationships, the process of networking begins with you in control—you are contacting specific individuals. As your network expands and you establish a set of professional relationships, your search for information or jobs will begin to move outside of your total control. A part of the networking process involves others assisting you by gathering information for you or recommending you as a possible job candidate. As additional people become a part of your networking system, you will have less knowledge about activities undertaken on your behalf; you will undoubtedly be contacted by individuals whom you did not initially approach. If you want to function effectively in surprise situations, you must be prepared at all times to talk with strangers about the informational or employment needs that motivated you to become involved in the networking process.

Preparing to Network

In deliberately establishing relationships, maximize your efforts by organizing your approach. Five specific areas in which you can organize your efforts include reviewing your self-assessment, reviewing your research on job sites and organizations, deciding who it is you want to talk to, keeping track of all your efforts, and creating your self-promotion tools.

Review Your Self-Assessment

Your self-assessment is as important a tool in preparing to network as it has been in other aspects of your job search. You have carefully evaluated your personal traits, personal values, economic needs, longer-term goals, skill base, preferred skills, and underdeveloped skills. During the networking process you will be called upon to communicate what you know about yourself and relate it to the information or job you seek. Be sure to review the exercises that you completed in the self-assessment section of this book in preparation for networking. We've explained that you need to assess what skills you have acquired from your major that are of general value to an employer and to be ready to express those in ways employers can appreciate as useful in their own organizations.

Review Researching Job Sites and Organizations

In addition, individuals assisting you will expect that you'll have at least some background information on the occupation or industry of interest to you. Refer to the appropriate sections of this book and other relevant publications to acquire the background information necessary for effective networking. They'll explain how to identify not only the job titles that might be of interest to you, but also what kinds of organizations employ people to do that job. You will develop some sense of working conditions and expectations about duties and responsibilities—all of which will be of help in your networking interviews.

Decide Who It Is You Want to Talk To

Networking cannot begin until you decide who it is that you want to talk to and, in general, what type of information you hope to gain from your contacts. Once you know this, it's time to begin developing a list of contacts. Five useful sources for locating contacts are described here.

College Alumni Network. Most colleges and universities have created a formal network of alumni and friends of the institution who are particularly interested in helping currently enrolled students and graduates of their alma mater gain employment-related information.

· ·

> Because the accounting major covers such a broad spectrum of human activity, you'll find accounting graduates employed in every sector of the economy: government, business, and nonprofit. The diversity of employment as evidenced by an alumni list from your college or university should be encouraging and informative. It's likely that you would enjoy talking with several among such a diversified group.

· ·

It is usually a simple process to make use of an alumni network. You need only visit the alumni or career office at your college or university and follow the procedure that has been established. Often, you will simply complete a form indicating your career goals and interests and you will be given the names of appropriate individuals to contact. In many cases, staff members will coach you on how to make the best use of the limited time these alumni contacts may have available for you.

Alumni networkers may provide some combination of the following services: day-long shadowing experiences, telephone interviews, in-person interviews, information on relocating to given geographic areas, internship information, suggestions on graduate school study, and job vacancy notices.

· ·

> What a valuable experience! Perhaps you are interested in working for a major corporation, but you are concerned about your degree preparation and whether your capabilities are up to the requirements of the particular firm. Spending a day with an alumnus who works for a similar enterprise, asking lots of questions about her educational training and preparation, will give you a more concrete view of the possibilities for your degree. Observing first-hand how this person does the job will be a far better deci-

sion criterion for you than any reading on the subject could possibly provide. In addition to your own observations, the alumnus will have her own perspective on the relevance of your training and will give you realistic and honest feedback on your job search concerns.

....

Present and Former Supervisors. If you believe you are on good terms with present or former job supervisors, they may be an excellent resource for providing information or directing you to appropriate resources that would have information related to your current interests and needs. Additionally, these supervisors probably belong to professional organizations, which they might be willing to utilize to get information for you.

....

If, for example, you were interested in working as an accountant with a major department store chain and you are currently working as an assistant in a local retail shop, talk with your supervisor or the owner. He may belong to the Chamber of Commerce, whose director would have information on local branches of the chain that are in need of help. You would then be able to obtain the names and telephone numbers of these people, thus enabling you to begin the networking process.

....

Employers in Your Area. Although you may be interested in working in a geographic location different from the one where you currently reside, don't overlook the value of the knowledge and contacts those around you are able to provide. Use the local telephone directory and newspaper to identify the types of organizations you are thinking of working for or professionals who have the kinds of jobs you are interested in. Recently, a call made to a local hospital's financial administrator for information on working in health care financial administration yielded more pertinent information on training seminars, regional professional organizations, and potential employment sites than a national organization was willing to provide.

Employers in Geographic Areas Where You Hope to Work. If you are thinking about relocating, identifying prospective employers or informational contacts in this new location will be critical to your success. Many resources are available to help you locate contact names. These include the yellow pages directory, the local newspapers, local or state business publications, and local Chambers of Commerce.

Professional Associations and Organizations. Professional associations and organizations can provide valuable information in several areas: career paths that you may not have considered, qualifications relating to those career choices, publications that list current job openings, and workshops or seminars that will enhance your professional knowledge and skills. They can also be excellent sources for background information on given industries: their health, current problems, and future challenges.

There are several excellent resources available to help you locate professional associations and organizations that would have information to meet your needs. Two especially useful publications are the *Encyclopedia of Associations* and the *National Trade and Professional Associations of the United States.*

Keep Track of All Your Efforts

It can be difficult, almost impossible, to remember all the details related to each contact you make during the networking process, so you will want to develop a record-keeping system that works for you. Formalize this process by using a notebook or index cards to organize the information you gather. Begin by creating a list of the people or organizations you want to contact. Record the contact's name, address, telephone number, and what information you hope to gain. Each entry might look something like this:

Contact Name	Address	Phone #	Purpose
Mr. Tim Keefe	Wrigley Bldg.		
Dir. of Mines	Suite 72	555-8906	Resume screen

Once you have created this initial list, it will be helpful to keep more detailed information as you begin to actually make the contacts. Using the Network Contact Record form in Exhibit 4.1, keep good information on all your network contacts. They'll appreciate your recall of details of your meetings and conversations, and the information will help you to focus your networking efforts.

Exhibit 4.1

Network Contact Record

Name: Be certain your spelling is absolutely correct.

Title: Pick up a business card to be certain of the correct title.

Employing organization: Note any parent company or subsidiaries.

Business mailing address: This is often different from the street address.

Business telephone number: Include area code/alternative numbers/fax.

Source for this contact: Who referred you, and what is their relationship?

Date of call or letter: Use plenty of space here to record multiple phone calls or visits, other employees you may have met, names of secretaries/receptionists, etc.

Content of discussion: Keep enough notes here to remind you of the substance of your visits and telephone conversations in case some time elapses between contacts.

Follow-up necessary to continue working with this contact: Your contact may request that you send them some materials or direct you to contact an associate. Note any such instructions or assignments in this space.

Name of additional networker: Here you would record the
Address: names and phone numbers of
Phone: additional contacts met at this
Name of additional networker: employer's site. Often you will
Address: be introduced to many people,
Phone: some of whom may indicate
Name of additional networker: a willingness to help in your
Address: job search.
Phone:

Date thank-you note written: May help to date your next contact.

Follow-up action taken: Phone calls, visits, additional notes.

continued

continued

Other miscellaneous notes: Record any other additional
interaction you may find is
important to remember in working
with this networking client. You will
want this form in front of you when
telephoning or just before and after
a visit.

Create Your Self-Promotion Tools

There are two types of promotional tools that are used in the networking process. The first is a resume and cover letter, and the second is a one-minute "infomercial," which may be given over the telephone or in person.

Techniques for writing an effective resume and cover letter are covered in Chapter 2. Once you have reviewed that material and prepared these important documents, you will have created one of your self-promotion tools.

The one-minute infomercial will demand that you begin tying your interests, abilities, and skills to the people or organizations you want to network with. Think about your goal for making the contact to help you understand what you should say about yourself. You should be able to express yourself easily and convincingly. If, for example, you are contacting an alumnus of your institution to obtain the names of possible employment sites in a distant city, be prepared to discuss why you are interested in moving to that location, the types of jobs you are interested in, and the skills and abilities you possess that will make you a qualified candidate.

To create a meaningful one-minute infomercial, write it out, practice it if it will be a spoken presentation, rewrite it, and practice it again if necessary until expressing yourself comes easily and is convincing.

Here's a simplified example of an infomercial for use over the telephone:

Hello, Mr. Pollard? My name is Sherry Douglas. I am a recent graduate of State College, and I wish to enter the healthcare field in accounting. I feel confident that I have many of the skills I understand are valued for accountants in healthcare. I have a strong quantitative background, with good investigative and computer skills. What's more, I have excellent interpersonal skills and work well under pressure. I understand these are valuable traits in this line of work!

Mr. Pollard, I'm calling you because I still need more information about accounting in the healthcare field. I'm hoping you'll have the time to sit down with me for about half an hour and discuss your perspective on accounting careers. There are so many possible places to get into accounting, and I am seeking some advice on which of those settings might be the best bet for my particular combination of skills and experience.

Would you be willing to do that for me? I would greatly appreciate it. I am available most mornings, if that's convenient for you.

....

Other effective self-promotion tools include portfolios for those in the arts, writing professions, or teaching. Portfolios show examples of work, photographs of projects or classroom activities, or certificates and credentials that are job related. There may not be an opportunity to use the portfolio during an interview, and it is not something that should be left with the organization. It is designed to be explained and displayed by the creator. However, during some networking meetings, there may be an opportunity to illustrate a point or strengthen a qualification by exhibiting the portfolio.

BEGINNING THE NETWORKING PROCESS

Set the Tone for Your Contacts

It can be useful to establish "tone words" for any communications you embark upon. Before making your first telephone call or writing your first letter, decide what you want your contact to think of you. If you are networking to try to obtain a job, your tone words might include words like *genuine, informed,* and *self-knowledgeable.* When trying to acquire information, your tone words may have a slightly different focus, such as *courteous, organized, focused,* and *well-spoken.* Use the tone words you establish for your contacts to guide you through the networking process.

Honestly Express Your Intentions

When contacting individuals, it is important to be honest about your reasons for making the contact. Establish your purpose in your own mind and be able and ready to articulate it concisely. Determine an initial agenda, whether it be informational questioning or self-promotion, present it to your contact, and be ready to respond immediately. If you don't adequately prepare before initiating your contacts, you may find yourself at a disadvantage if you're asked to immediately begin your informational interview or self-promotion during the first phone conversation or visit.

Start Networking Within Your Circle of Confidence

Once you have organized your approach—by utilizing specific researching methods, creating a system for keeping track of the people you will contact, and developing effective self-promotion tools—you are ready to begin networking. The best place to begin networking is by talking with a group of people you trust and feel comfortable with. This group is usually made up of your family, friends, and career counselors. No matter who is in this inner circle, they will have a special interest in seeing you succeed in your job search. In addition, because they will be easy to talk to, you should try taking some risks in terms of practicing your information-seeking approach. Gain confidence in talking about the strengths you bring to an organization and the underdeveloped skills you feel hinder your candidacy. Be sure to review the section on self-assessment for tips on approaching each of these areas. Ask for critical but constructive feedback from the people in your circle of confidence on the letters you write and the one-minute infomercial you have developed. Evaluate whether you want to make the changes they suggest, then practice the changes on others within this circle.

Stretch the Boundaries of Your Networking Circle of Confidence

Once you have refined the promotional tools you will use to accomplish your networking goals, you will want to make additional contacts. Because you will not know most of these people, it will be a less comfortable activity to undertake. The practice that you gained with your inner circle of trusted friends should have prepared you to now move outside of that comfort zone.

It is said that any information a person needs is only two phone calls away, but the information cannot be gained until you (1) make a reasonable guess about who might have the information you need and (2) pick up the telephone to make the call. Using your network list that includes alumni, instructors, supervisors, employers, and associations, you can begin preparing your list of questions that will allow you to get the information you need. Review the question list shown below and then develop a list of your own.

Questions You Might Want to Ask

1. In the position you now hold, what do you do on a typical day?

2. What are the most interesting aspects of your job?

3. What part of your work do you consider dull or repetitious?

4. What were the jobs you had that led to your present position?

5. How long does it usually take to move from one step to the next in this career path?

6. What is the top position to which you can aspire in this career path?

7. What is the next step in your career path?

8. Are there positions in this field that are similar to your position?

9. What are the required qualifications and training for entry-level positions in this field?

10. Are there specific courses a student should take to be qualified to work in this field?

11. What are the entry-level jobs in this field?

12. What types of training are provided to persons entering this field?

13. What are the salary ranges your organization typically offers to entry-level candidates for positions in this field?

14. What special advice would you give a person entering this field?

15. Do you see this field as a growing one?

16. How do you see the content of the entry-level jobs in this field changing over the next two years?

17. What can I do to prepare myself for these changes?

18. What is the best way to obtain a position that will start me on a career in this field?

19. Do you have any information on job specifications and descriptions that I may have?

20. What related occupational fields would you suggest I explore?

21. How could I improve my resume for a career in this field?

22. Who else would you suggest I talk to, both in your organization and in other organizations?

Questions You Might Have to Answer

In order to communicate effectively, you must anticipate questions that will be asked of you by the networkers you contact. Review the list below and see if you can easily answer each of these questions. If you cannot, it may be time to revisit the self-assessment process.

1. Where did you get my name, or how did you find out about this organization?

2. What are your career goals?

3. What kind of job are you interested in?

4. What do you know about this organization and this industry?

5. How do you know you're prepared to undertake an entry-level position in this industry?

6. What course work have you taken that is related to your career interests?

7. What are your short-term career goals?

8. What are your long-term career goals?

9. Do you plan to obtain additional formal education?

10. What contributions have you made to previous employers?

11. Which of your previous jobs have you enjoyed the most, and why?

12. What are you particularly good at doing?

13. What shortcomings have you had to face in previous employment?

14. What are your three greatest strengths?

15. Describe how comfortable you feel with your communication style.

General Networking Tips

Make Every Contact Count. Setting the tone for each interaction is critical. Approaches that will help you communicate in an effective way include politeness, being appreciative of time provided to you, and being prepared and thorough. Remember, *everyone* within an organization has a circle of influence, so be prepared to interact effectively with each person you encounter in the networking process, including secretarial and support staff. Many information or job seekers have thwarted their own efforts by being rude to some individuals they encountered as they networked because they made the incorrect assumption that certain persons were unimportant.

Sometimes your contacts may be surprised at their ability to help you. After meeting and talking with you, they might think they have not offered much in the way of help. A day or two later, however, they may make a contact that would be useful to you and refer you to it.

With Each Contact, Widen Your Circle of Networkers. Always leave an informational interview with the names of at least two more people who can help you get the information or job that you are seeking. Don't be shy about asking for additional contacts; networking is all about increasing the number of people you can interact with to achieve your goals.

Make Your Own Decisions. As you talk with different people and get answers to the questions you pose, you may hear conflicting information or get conflicting suggestions. Your job is to listen to these "experts" and decide what information and which suggestions will help you achieve *your* goals. Only implement those suggestions that you believe will work for you.

SHUTTING DOWN YOUR NETWORK

As you achieve the goals that motivated your networking activity—getting the information you need or the job you want—the time will come to inactivate all or parts of your network. As you do so, be sure to tell your primary supporters about your change in status. Call or write to each one of them and give them as many details about your new status as you feel is necessary to maintain a positive relationship.

Because a network takes on a life of its own, activity undertaken on your behalf will continue even after you cease your efforts. As you get calls or are contacted in some fashion, be sure to inform these networkers about your change in status, and thank them for assistance they have provided.

Information on the latest employment trends indicates that workers will change jobs or careers several times in their lifetime. If you carefully and thoughtfully conduct your networking activities now, you will have solid experience when you need to network again.

CHAPTER FIVE

INTERVIEWING

*C*ertainly, there can be no one part of the job search process more fraught with anxiety and worry than the interview. Yet seasoned job seekers welcome the interview and will often say, "Just get me an interview and I'm on my way!" They understand that the interview is crucial to the hiring process and equally crucial for them, as job candidates, to have the opportunity of a personal dialogue to add to what the employer may already have learned from a resume, cover letter, and telephone conversations.

Believe it or not, the interview is to be welcomed, and even enjoyed! It is a perfect opportunity for you, the candidate, to sit down with an employer and express yourself and display who you are and what you want. Of course, it takes thought and planning and a little strategy; after all, it *is* a job interview! But it can be a positive, if not pleasant, experience and one you can look back on and feel confident about your performance and effort.

For many new job seekers, a job, any job, seems a wonderful thing. But seasoned interview veterans know that the job interview is an important step for both sides—the employer and the candidate—to see what each has to offer and whether there is going to be a "fit" of personalities, work styles, and attitudes. And it is this concept of balance in the interview, that both sides have important parts to play, that holds the key to success in mastering this aspect of the job search strategy.

Try to think of the interview as a conversation between two interested and equal partners. You both have important, even vital, information to deliver and to learn. Of course, there's no denying the employer has some leverage, especially in the initial interview for recruitment or any interview scheduled by the candidate and not the recruiter. That should not prevent the interviewee from seeking to play an equal part in what should be a fair exchange of information. Too often the untutored candidate allows the interview to become one-sided. The employer asks all the questions and the candidate simply responds. The ideal would be for two mutually interested parties to sit down and discuss possibilities for each. For this is a *conversation of signifi-*

cance, and it requires pre-interview preparation, thought about the tone of the interview, and planning of the nature and details of the information to be exchanged.

PREPARING FOR THE INTERVIEW

Most initial interviews are about thirty minutes long. Given the brevity, the information that is exchanged ought to be important. The candidate should be delivering material that the employer cannot discover on the resume and, in turn, the candidate should be learning things about the employer that he or she could not otherwise find out. After all, if you have only thirty minutes, why waste time on information that is already published? The information exchanged is more than just factual, and both sides will learn much from what they see of each other, as well. How the candidate looks, speaks, and acts is important to the employer. The employer's attention to the interview and awareness of the candidate's resume, the setting, and the quality of information presented are important to the candidate.

Just as the employer has every right to be disappointed when a prospect is late for the interview, looks unkempt, and seems ill-prepared to answer fairly standard questions, the candidate may be disappointed with an interviewer who isn't ready for the meeting, hasn't learned the basic resume facts, and is constantly interrupted for telephone calls. In either situation, there's good reason to feel let down.

There are many elements to a successful interview, and some of them are not easy to describe or prepare for. Sometimes there is just a chemistry between interviewer and interviewee that brings out the best in both, and a good exchange takes place. But there is much the candidate can do to pave the way for success in terms of his or her resume, personal appearance, goals, and interview strategy—each of which we will discuss. However, none of this preparation is as important as the time and thought the candidate gives to personal self-assessment.

Self-Assessment

Neither a stunning resume nor an expensive, well-tailored suit can compensate for candidates who do not know what they want, where they are going, or why they are interviewing with a particular employer. Self-assessment, the process by which we begin to know and acknowledge our own particular blend of education, experiences, needs, and goals is not something that can be sorted out the weekend before a major interview. Of all the elements of interview preparation, this one requires the longest lead time and cannot be faked.

Because the time allotted for most interviews is brief, it is all the more important for job candidates to understand and express succinctly why they are there and what they have to offer. This is not a time for undue modesty or for braggadocio, either; but it is a time for a compelling, reasoned statement of why you feel that you and this employer might make a good match. It means you have to have thought about your skills, interests, and attributes; related those to your life experiences and your own history of challenges and opportunities; and determined what that indicates about your strengths, preferences, values, and areas needing further development.

A common complaint of employers is that many candidates didn't take advantage of the interview time, didn't seem to know why they were there or what they wanted. When asked to talk about themselves and their work-related skills and attributes, employers don't want to be faced with shyness or embarrassed laughter; they need to know about you so they can make a fair determination of you and your competition. If you lose the opportunity to make a case for your employability, you can be certain the person ahead of you has or the person after you will, and it will be on the strength of those impressions that the employer will hire.

If you need some assistance with self-assessment issues, refer to Chapter 1. Included are suggested exercises that can be done as needed, such as making up an experiential diary and extracting obvious strengths and weaknesses from past experiences. These simple, pen-and-paper assignments will help you look at past activities as collections of tasks with accompanying skills and responsibilities. Don't overlook your high school or college career office, as well. Many offer personal counseling on self-assessment issues and may provide testing instruments such as the Myers-Briggs Type Indicator (MBTI)®, the Harrington-O'Shea Career Decision Making® System (CDM), the Strong Interest Inventory (SII)®, or any of a wide selection of assessment tools that can help you clarify some of these issues prior to the interview stage of your job search.

The Resume

Resume preparation has been discussed in detail, and some basic examples of various types were provided. In this section, we want to concentrate on how best to use your resume in the interview. In most cases, the employer will have seen the resume prior to the interview, and, in fact, it may well have been the quality of that resume that secured the interview opportunity.

An interview is a conversation, however, and not an exercise in reading. So, if the employer hasn't seen your resume and you have brought it along to the interview, wait until asked or until the end of the interview to offer it. Otherwise, you may find yourself staring at the back of your resume and simply answering "yes" and "no" to a series of questions drawn from that document.

Sometimes an interviewer is not prepared and does not know or recall the contents of the resume and may use the resume to a greater or lesser degree as a "prompt" during the interview. It is for you to judge what that may indicate about the individual doing the interview or the employer. If your interviewer seems surprised by the scheduled meeting, relies on the resume to an inordinate degree, and seems otherwise unfamiliar with your background, this lack of preparation for the hiring process could well be a symptom of general management disorganization or may simply be the result of poor planning on the part of one individual. It is your responsibility as a potential employee to be aware of these signals and make your decisions accordingly.

....

In any event, it is perfectly acceptable for you to get the conversation back to a more interpersonal style by saying something like, "Mr. Smith, you might be interested in some recent accounting experience I gained in an internship that is not detailed on my resume. May I tell you about it?" This can return the interview to two people talking to each other, not one reading and the other responding.

....

By all means, bring at least one copy of your resume to the interview. Occasionally, at the close of an interview, an interviewer will express an interest in circulating a resume to several departments, and you could then offer to provide those. Sometimes, an interview appointment provides an opportunity to meet others in the organization who may express an interest in you and your background, and it may be helpful to follow that up with a copy of your resume. Our best advice, however, is to keep it out of sight until needed or requested.

Appearance

Although many of the absolute rules that once dominated the advice offered to job candidates about appearance have now been moderated significantly, conservative is still the watchword unless you are interviewing in a fashion-related industry. For men, conservative translates into a well-cut dark suit with appropriate tie, hosiery, and dress shirt. A wise strategy for the male job seeker looking for a good but not expensive suit would be to try the men's department of a major department store. They usually carry a good range of sizes, fabrics, and prices; offer professional sales help; provide free tailoring; and have associated departments for putting together a professional look.

For women, there is more latitude. Business suits are still popular, but they have become more feminine in color and styling with a variety of jacket and skirt lengths. In addition to suits, better-quality dresses are now worn in many environments and, with the correct accessories, can be most appropriate. Company literature, professional magazines, the business section of major newspapers, and television interviews can all give clues about what is being worn in different employer environments.

Both men and women need to pay attention to issues such as hair, jewelry, and make-up; these are often what separates the candidate in appearance from the professional work force. It seems particularly difficult for the young job seeker to give up certain hair styles, eyeglass fashions, and jewelry habits, yet those can be important to the employer, who is concerned with your ability to successfully make the transition into the organization. Candidates often find the best strategy is to dress conservatively until they find employment. Once employed and familiar with the norms within your organization, you can begin to determine a look that you enjoy, works for you, and fits your organization.

Choose clothes that suit your body type, fit well, and flatter you. Feel good about the way you look! The interview day is not the best for a new hairdo, a new pair of shoes, or any other change that will distract you or cause you to be self-conscious. Arrive a bit early to avoid being rushed, and ask the receptionist to direct you to a restroom for any last-minute adjustments of hair and clothes.

Employer Information

Whether your interview is for graduate school admission, an overseas corporate position, or a reporter position with a local newspaper, it is important to know something about the employer or the organization. Keeping in mind that the interview is relatively brief and that you will hopefully have other interviews with other organizations, it is important to keep your research in proportion. If secondary interviews are called for, you will have additional time to do further research. For the first interview, it is helpful to know the organization's mission, goals, size, scope of operations, etc. Your research may uncover recent areas of challenge or particular successes that may help to fuel the interview. Use the "Where Are These Jobs, Anyway?" section of Chapter 3, your library, and your career or guidance office to help you locate this information in the most efficient way possible. Don't be shy in asking advice of these counseling and guidance professionals on how best to spend your preparation time. With some practice, you'll soon learn how much information is enough and which kinds of information are most useful to you.

INTERVIEW CONTENT

We've already discussed how it can help to think of the interview as an important conversation—one that, as with any conversation, you want to find pleasant and interesting and leaves you with a good feeling. But because this conversation is especially important, the information that's exchanged is critical to its success. What do you want them to know about you? What do you need to know about them? What interview technique do you need to particularly pay attention to? How do you want to manage the close of the interview? What steps will follow in the hiring process?

Except for the professional interviewer, most of us find interviewing stressful and anxiety-provoking. Developing a strategy before you begin interviewing will help you relieve some stress and anxiety. One particular strategy that has worked for many and may work for you is interviewing by objective. Before you interview, write down three to five goals you would like to achieve for that interview. They may be technique goals: smile a little more, have a firmer handshake, be sure to ask about the next stage in the interview process before leaving, etc. They may be content-oriented goals: find out about the company's current challenges and opportunities, be sure to speak of my recent research writing experiences or foreign travel, etc. Whatever your goals, jot down a few of them as goals for this interview.

Most people find that, in trying to achieve these few goals, their interviewing technique becomes more organized and focused. After the interview, the most common question friends and family ask is, "How did it go?" With this technique, you have an indication of whether you met *your* goals for the meeting, not just some vague idea of how it went. Chances are, if you accomplished what you wanted to, it informed the quality of the entire interview. As you continue to interview, you will want to revise your goals to continue improving your interview skills.

Now, add to the concept of the significant conversation the idea of a beginning, a middle, and a closing and you will have two thoughts that will give your interview a distinctive character. Be sure to make your introduction warm and cordial. Say your full name (and if it's a difficult-to-pronounce name, help the interviewer to pronounce it) and make certain you know your interviewer's name and how to pronounce it. Most interviews begin with some "soft talk" about the weather, chat about the candidate's trip to the interview site, national events, etc. This is done as a courtesy, to relax both you and the interviewer, to get you talking, and to generally try to defuse the atmosphere of excessive tension. Try to be yourself, engage in the conversation, and don't try to second-guess the interviewer. This is simply what it appears to be—casual conversation.

Once you and the interviewer move on to exchange more serious information in the middle part of the interview, the two most important concerns become your ability to handle challenging questions and your success at asking meaningful ones. Interviewer questions will probably fall into one of three categories: personal assessment and career direction, academic background, and knowledge of the employer. The following are some examples of questions in each category:

Personal Assessment and Career Direction

1. How would you describe yourself?
2. What motivates you to put forth your greatest effort?
3. In what kind of work environment are you most comfortable?
4. What do you consider to be your greatest strengths and weaknesses?
5. How well do you work under pressure?
6. What qualifications do you have that make you think you will be successful in this career?
7. Will you relocate? What do you feel would be the most difficult aspect of relocating?
8. Are you willing to travel?
9. Why should I hire you?

Academic Assessment

1. Why did you select your college or university?
2. What changes would you make at your alma mater?
3. What led you to choose your major?
4. What subjects did you like best and least? Why?
5. If you could, how would you plan your academic study differently? Why?
6. Describe your most rewarding college experience.
7. How has your college experience prepared you for this career?
8. Do you think that your grades are a good indication of your ability to succeed with this organization?
9. Do you have plans for continued study?

Knowledge of the Employer

1. If you were hiring a graduate of your school for this position, what qualities would you look for?

2. What do you think it takes to be successful in an organization like ours?

3. In what ways do you think you can make a contribution to our organization?

4. Why did you choose to seek a position with this organization?

The interviewer wants a response to each question but is also gauging your enthusiasm, preparedness, and willingness to communicate. In each response you should provide some information about yourself that can be related to the employer's needs. A common mistake is to give too much information. Answer each question completely, but be careful not to run on too long with extensive details or examples.

Questions About Underdeveloped Skills

Most employers interview people who have met some minimum criteria of education and experience. They interview candidates to see who they are, to learn what kind of personality they exhibit, and to get some sense of how this person might fit into the existing organization. It may be that you are asked about skills the employer hopes to find and that you have not documented. Maybe it's grant-writing experience, knowledge of the European political system, or a knowledge of the film world.

To questions about skills and experiences you don't have, answer honestly and forthrightly and try to offer some additional information about skills you do have. For example, perhaps the employer is disappointed you have no grant-writing experience. An honest answer may be as follows:

> No, unfortunately, I was never in a position to acquire those skills. I do understand something of the complexities of the grant-writing process and feel confident that my attention to detail, careful reading skills, and strong writing would make grants a wonderful challenge in a new job. I think I could get up on the learning curve quickly.

The employer hears an honest admission of lack of experience but is reassured by some specific skill details that do relate to grant writing and a confident manner that suggests enthusiasm and interest in a challenge.

For many students, questions about their possible contribution to an employer's organization can prove challenging. Because your education has probably not included specific training for a job, you need to review your academic record and select capabilities you have developed in your major that an employer can appreciate. For example, perhaps you read well and can analyze and condense what you've read into smaller, more focused pieces. That could be valuable. Or maybe you did some serious research and you know you have valuable investigative skills. Your public speaking might be highly developed and you might use visual aids appropriately and effectively. Or maybe your skill at correspondence, memos, and messages is effective. Whatever it is, you must take it out of the academic context and put it into a new, employer-friendly context so your interviewer can best judge how you could help the organization.

Exhibiting knowledge of the organization will, without a doubt, show the interviewer that you are interested enough in the available position to have done some legwork in preparation for the interview. Remember, it is not necessary to know every detail of the organization's history, but rather to have a general knowledge about why it is in business and how the industry is faring.

Sometime during the interview, generally after the midway point, you'll be asked if you have any questions for the interviewer. Your questions will tell the employer much about your attitude and your desire to understand the organization's expectations so you can compare it to your own strengths. The following are some selected questions you might want to ask:

1. What are the main responsibilities of the position?

2. What are the opportunities and challenges associated with this position?

3. Could you outline some possible career paths beginning with this position?

4. How regularly do performance evaluations occur?

5. What is the communication style of the organization? (meetings, memos, etc.)

6. Describe a typical day for me in this position.

7. What kinds of opportunities might exist for me to improve my professional skills within the organization?

8. What have been some of the interesting challenges and opportunities your organization has recently faced?

Most interviews draw to a natural closing point, so be careful not to prolong the discussion. At a signal from the interviewer, wind up your presentation, express your appreciation for the opportunity, and be sure to ask what the next stage in the process will be. When can you expect to hear from them?

Will they be conducting second-tier interviews? If you're interested and haven't heard, would they mind a phone call? Be sure to collect a business card with the name and phone number of your interviewer. On your way out, you might have an opportunity to pick up organizational literature you haven't seen before.

With the right preparation—a thorough self-assessment, professional clothing, and employer information—you'll be able to set and achieve the goals you have established for the interview process.

CHAPTER SIX

NETWORKING OR INTERVIEWING FOLLOW-UP

Quite often, there is a considerable time lag between interviewing for a position and being hired, or, in the case of the networker, between your phone call or letter to a possible contact and the opportunity of a meeting. This can be frustrating. "Why aren't they contacting me?" "I thought I'd get another interview, but no one has telephoned." "Am I out of the running?" You don't know what is happening.

CONSIDER THE DIFFERING PERSPECTIVES

Of course, there is another perspective—that of the networker or hiring organization. Organizations are complex, with multiple tasks that need to be accomplished each day. Hiring is but one discrete activity that does not occur as frequently as other job assignments. The hiring process might have to take second place to other, more immediate organizational needs. Although it may be very important to you and it is certainly ultimately significant to the employer, other issues such as fiscal management, planning and product development, employer vacation periods, or financial constraints, may prevent an organization or individual within that organization from acting on your employment or your request for information as quickly as you or they would prefer.

USE YOUR COMMUNICATION SKILLS

Good communication is essential here to resolve any anxieties, and the responsibility is on you, the job or information seeker. Too many job seekers and networkers offer as an excuse that they don't want to "bother" the organization by writing letters or calling. Let us assure you here and now, once and for all, that if you are troubling an organization by over-communicating, someone will indicate that situation to you quite clearly. If not, you can only assume you are a worthwhile prospect and the employer appreciates being reminded of your availability and interest in them. Let's look at follow-up practices in both the job interview process and the networking situation separately.

FOLLOWING UP ON THE EMPLOYMENT INTERVIEW

A brief thank-you note following an interview is an excellent and polite way to begin a series of follow-up communications with a potential employer with whom you have interviewed and want to remain in touch. It should be just that—a thank you for a good meeting. If you failed to mention some fact or experience during your interview that you think might add to your candidacy, you may use this note to do that. However, this should be essentially a note whose overall tone is appreciative and, if appropriate, indicative of a continuing interest in pursuing any opportunity that may exist with that organization. It is one of the few pieces of business correspondence that may be handwritten, but always use plain, good quality, monarch-size paper.

If, however, at this point you are no longer interested in the employer, the thank-you note is an appropriate time to indicate that. You are under no obligation to identify any reason for not continuing to pursue employment with that organization, but if you are so inclined to indicate your professional reasons (pursuing other employers more akin to your interests, looking for greater income production than this employer can provide, a different geographic location than is available, etc.), you certainly may. It should not be written with an eye to negotiation, for it will not be interpreted as such.

As part of your interview closing, you should have taken the initiative to establish lines of communication for continuing information about your candidacy. If you asked permission to telephone, wait a week following your thank-you note, then telephone your contact simply to inquire how things are progressing on your employment status. The feedback you receive here should be taken at face value. If your interviewer simply has no information, he or she will tell you so and indicate whether you should call again and when. Don't be discouraged if this should continue over some period of time.

If during this time something occurs that you think improves or changes your candidacy (some new qualification or experience you may have had), including any offers from other organizations, by all means telephone or write to inform the employer about this. In the case of an offer from a competing but less desirable or equally desirable organization, telephone your contact, explain what has happened, express your real interest in the organization, and inquire whether some determination on your employment might be made before you must respond to this other offer. If the organization is truly interested in you, they may be moved to make a decision about your candidacy. Equally possible is the scenario in which they are not yet ready to make a decision and so advise you to take the offer that has been presented. Again, you have no ethical alternative but to deal with the information presented in a straightforward manner.

When accepting other employment, be sure to contact any employers still actively considering you and inform them of your new job. Thank them graciously for their consideration. There are many other job seekers out there just like you who will benefit from having their candidacy improved when others bow out of the race. Who knows, you might, at some future time, have occasion to interact professionally with one of the organizations with whom you sought employment. How embarrassing to have someone remember you as the candidate who failed to notify them of taking a job elsewhere!

In all of your follow-up communications, keep good notes of who you spoke with, when you called, and any instructions that were given about return communications. This will prevent any misunderstandings and provide you with good records of what has transpired.

FOLLOWING UP ON THE NETWORK CONTACT

Far more common than the forgotten follow-up after an interview is the situation where a good network contact is allowed to lapse. Good communications are the essence of a network, and follow-up is not so much a matter of courtesy here as it is a necessity. In networking for job information and contacts, you are the active network link. Without you, and without continual contact from you, there is no network. You and your need for employment is often the only shared element between members of the network. Because network contacts were made regardless of the availability of any particular employment, it is incumbent upon the job seeker, if not simple common sense, that unless you stay in regular communication with the network, you will not be available for consideration should some job become available in the future.

This brings up the issue of responsibility, which is likewise very clear. The job seeker initiates network contacts and is responsible for maintaining those contacts; therefore, the entire responsibility for the network belongs with him or her. This becomes patently obvious if the network is left unattended. It very shortly falls out of existence, as it cannot survive without careful attention by the networker.

A variety of ways are open to you to keep the lines of communication open and to attempt to interest the network in you as a possible employee. You are limited only by your own enthusiasm for members of the network and your creativity. However, you as a networker are well-advised to keep good records of whom you have met and spoken with in each organization. Be sure to send thank-you notes to anyone who has spent any time with you, be it a quick tour of a department or a sit-down informational interview. All of these communications should, in addition to their ostensible reason, add some information about you and your particular combination of strengths and attributes.

You can contact your network at any time to convey continued interest, to comment on some recent article you came across concerning an organization, to add information about your training or changes in your qualifications, to ask advice or seek guidance in your job search, or to request referrals to other possible network opportunities. Sometimes just a simple note to network members reminding them of your job search, indicating that you have been using their advice, and noting that you are still actively pursuing leads and hope to continue to interact with them is enough to keep communications alive.

Because networks have been abused in the past, it's important that your conduct be above reproach. Networks are exploratory options, they are not back-door access to employers. The network works best for someone who is exploring a new industry or making a transition into a new area of employment and who needs to find information or to alert people to their search activity. Always be candid and direct with contacts in expressing the purpose of your call or letter and your interest in their help or information about their organization. In follow-up contacts, keep the tone professional and direct. Your honesty will be appreciated, and people will respond as best they can if your qualifications appear to meet their forthcoming needs. The network does not owe you anything, and that tone should be clear to each person you meet.

FEEDBACK FROM FOLLOW-UPS

A network contact may prove to be miscalculated. Perhaps you were referred to someone and it became clear that your goals and their particular needs did not make a good match. Or the network contact may simply not be in a position to provide you with the information you are seeking. Or in some unfortunate situations, the contact may become annoyed by being contacted for this purpose. In such a situation, many job seekers simply say "Thank you" and move on.

If the contact is simply not the right contact, but the individual you are speaking with is not annoyed by the call, it might be a better tactic to express regret that the contact was misplaced and then express to the contact what you are seeking and ask for their advice or possible suggestions as to a next step. The more people who are aware you are seeking employment, the better your chances of connecting, and that is the purpose of a network. Most people in a profession have excellent knowledge of their field and varying amounts of expertise on areas near to or tangent to their own. Use their expertise and seek some guidance before you dissolve the contact. You may be pleasantly surprised.

Occasionally, networkers will express the feeling that they have done as much as they can or provided all the information that is available to them. This may be a cue that they would like to be released from your network. Be alert to such attempts to terminate, graciously thank the individual by letter, and move on in your network development. A network is always changing, adding and losing members, and you want the network to be composed of only those who are actively interested in supporting your interests.

A FINAL POINT ON NETWORKING FOR ACCOUNTING MAJORS

In any of the settings you might consider as a potential place to work, your contacts will be critically evaluating all of your written and oral communications. This should serve to emphasize the importance of the quality of your interactions with people in a position to help you in your job search.

In your telephone communications, interview presentation, and follow-up correspondence, your warmth, style, and personality as evidenced in your spoken and written use of English will be part of the portfolio of impressions you create just as much as your accounting ability.

CHAPTER SEVEN

JOB OFFER CONSIDERATIONS

f or many recent college graduates, the thrill of their first job and, for some, the most substantial regular income they have ever earned seems an excess of good fortune coming at once. To question that first income or be critical in any way of the conditions of employment at the time of the initial offer seems like looking a gift horse in the mouth. It doesn't seem to occur to many new hires even to attempt to negotiate any aspect of their first job. And, as many employers who deal with entry-level jobs for recent college graduates will readily confirm, the reality is that there simply isn't much movement in salary available to these new college recruits. The entry-level hire generally does not have an employment track record on a professional level to provide any leverage for negotiation. Real negotiations on salary, benefits, retirement provisions, etc., come to those with significant employment records at higher income levels.

Of course, the job offer is more than just money. It can be comprised of geographic assignment, duties and responsibilities, training, benefits, health and medical insurance, educational assistance, car allowance or company vehicle, and a host of other items. All of this is generally detailed in the formal letter that presents the final job offer. In most cases, this is a follow-up to a personal phone call from the employer representative who has been principally responsible for your hiring process.

That initial telephone offer is certainly binding as a verbal agreement, but most firms follow up with a detailed letter outlining the most significant parts of your employment contract. You may certainly choose to respond immediately at the time of the telephone offer (which would be considered a binding oral contract), but you will also be required to formally answer the letter of offer with a letter of acceptance, restating the salient elements of the employer's description of your position, salary, and benefits. This ensures that both parties are clear on the terms and conditions of employment and remuneration and any other outstanding aspects of the job offer.

IS THIS THE JOB YOU WANT?

Most new employees will write this letter of acceptance back, glad to be in the position to accept employment. If you've worked hard to get the offer, and the job market is tight, other offers may not be in sight, so you will say "Yes, I accept!" What is important here is that the job offer you accept be one that does fit your particular needs, values, and interests as you've outlined them in your self-assessment process. Moreover, it should be a job that will not only use your skills and education, but also challenge you to develop new skills and talents.

Jobs are sometimes accepted too hastily, for the wrong reasons, and without proper scrutiny by the applicant. For example, an individual might readily accept a sales job only to find the continual rejection by potential clients unendurable. An office worker might realize within weeks the constraints of a desk job and yearn for more activity. Employment is an important part of our lives. It is, for most of our adult lives, our most continuous productive activity. We want to make good choices based on the right criteria.

If you have a low tolerance for risk, a job based on commission will certainly be very anxiety provoking. If being near your family is important, issues of relocation could present a decision crisis for you. If you're an adventurous person, a job with frequent travel would provide needed excitement and be very desirable. The importance of income, the need to continue your education, your personal health situation—all of these have an impact on whether the job you are considering will ultimately meet your needs. Unless you've spent some time understanding and thinking about these issues, it will be difficult to evaluate offers you do receive.

More importantly, if you make a decision that you cannot tolerate and feel you must leave that job, you will then have both unemployment and self-esteem issues to contend with. These will combine to make the next job search tough going, indeed. So make your acceptance a carefully considered decision.

NEGOTIATING YOUR OFFER

It may be that there is some aspect of your job offer that is not particularly attractive to you. Perhaps there is no relocation allotment to help you move your possessions, and this presents some financial hardship for you. It may be that the medical and health insurance is less than you had hoped. Your initial assignment may be different than you expected, either in its location or in the duties and responsibilities that comprise it. Or it may simply be that the salary is less than you anticipated. Other considerations may be your official starting date of employment, vacation time, evening hours, dates of training programs or schools, etc.

If you are considering not accepting the job because of some item or items in the job offer "package" that do not meet your needs, you should know that most employers emphatically wish that you would bring that issue to their attention. It may be that the employer can alter it to make the offer more agreeable for you. In some cases, it cannot be changed. In any event, the employer would generally like to have the opportunity to try to remedy a difficulty rather than risk losing a good potential employee over an issue that might have been resolved. After all, they have spent time and funds in securing your services, and they certainly deserve an opportunity to resolve any possible differences.

Honesty is the best approach in discussing any objections or uneasiness you might have over the employer's offer. Having received your formal offer in writing, contact your employer representative and indicate your particular dissatisfaction in a straightforward manner. For example, you might explain that, while very interested in being employed by this organization, the salary (or any other benefit) is less than you have determined you require. State the terms you do need, and listen to the response. You may be asked to put this in writing, or you may be asked to hold off until the firm can decide on a response. If you are dealing with a senior representative of the organization, one who has been involved in hiring for some time, you may get an immediate response or a solid indication of possible outcomes.

Perhaps the issue is one of relocation. Your initial assignment is in the Midwest, and because you had indicated a strong West Coast preference, you are surprised at the actual assignment. You might simply indicate that, while you understand the need for the company to assign you based on its needs, you are disappointed and had hoped to be placed on the West Coast. You could inquire if that were still possible and, if not, would it be reasonable to expect a West Coast relocation in the future.

If your request is presented in a reasonable way, the employer will not see this as jeopardizing your offer. If they can agree to your proposal, they will. If not, they will simply tell you so, and you may choose to continue your candidacy with them or remove yourself from consideration as a possible employee. The choice will be up to you.

Some firms will adjust benefits within their parameters to meet the candidate's need if at all possible. If a candidate requires a relocation cost allowance, he or she may be asked to forgo tuition benefits for the first year to accomplish this adjustment. An increase in life insurance may be adjusted by some other benefit trade-off; perhaps a family dental plan is not needed. In these decisions, you are called upon, sometimes under time pressure, to know how you value these issues and how important each is to you.

Many employers find they are more comfortable negotiating for candidates who have unique qualifications or who bring especially needed expertise to the organization. Employers hiring large numbers of entry-level college graduates may be far more reluctant to accommodate any changes in offer conditions. They are well supplied with candidates with similar education and experience, so that if rejected by one candidate, they can draw new candidates from an ample labor pool.

COMPARING OFFERS

With only about 40 percent of recent college graduates employed three months after graduation, many graduates do not get to enjoy the experience of entertaining more than one offer at a time. The conditions of the economy, the job seekers' particular geographic job market, and their own needs and demands for certain employment conditions may not provide more than one offer at a time. Some job seekers may feel that no reasonable offer should go unaccepted, for the simple fear there won't be another.

In a tough job market, or if the job you seek is not widely available, or when your job search goes on too long and becomes difficult to sustain financially and emotionally, it may be necessary to accept an offer. The alternative is continued unemployment. Even here, when you feel you don't have a choice, you can at least understand that in accepting this particular offer, there may be limitations and conditions you don't appreciate. At the time of acceptance, there were no other alternatives, but the new employee can begin to use that position to gain the experience and talent to move toward a more attractive position.

Sometimes, however, more than one offer is received at one time, and the candidate has the luxury of choice. If the job seeker knows what he or she wants and has done the necessary self-assessment honestly and thoroughly, it may be clear that one of the offers conforms more closely to those expressed wants and needs.

However, if, as so often happens, the offers are similar in terms of conditions and salary, the question then becomes which organization might provide the necessary climate, opportunities, and advantages for your professional development and growth. This is the time when solid employer research and astute questioning during the interviews really pays off. How much did you learn about the employer through your own research and skillful questioning? When the interviewer asked during the interview, "Do you have any questions?" did you ask the kinds of questions that would help resolve a choice between one organization and another? Just as an employer must decide among numerous applicants, so must the applicant learn to assess the potential employer. Both are partners in the job search.

RENEGING ON AN OFFER

An especially disturbing occurrence for employers and career counseling professionals is when a job seeker formally (either orally or by written contract) accepts employment with one organization and later reneges on the agreement and goes with another employer.

There are all kinds of rationalizations offered for this unethical behavior. None of them satisfies. The sad irony is that what the job seeker is willing to do to the employer—make a promise and then break it—he or she would be outraged to have done to them—have the job offer pulled. It is a very bad way to begin a career. It suggests the individual has not taken the time to do the necessary self-assessment and self-awareness exercises to think and judge critically. The new offer taken may, in fact, be no better or worse than the one refused. Job candidates should be aware that there have been incidents of legal action following job candidates reneging on an offer. This adds a very sour note to what should be a harmonious beginning of a lifelong adventure.

CHAPTER EIGHT

THE GRADUATE SCHOOL CHOICE

The reasons for continuing one's education in graduate school can be as varied and unique as the individuals electing this course of action. Many continue their studies at an advanced level because they simply find it difficult to end the educational process. They love what they are learning and want to learn more and continue their academic exploration.

• •

Continuing to work with a particular subject, such as the dynamics of organizational behavior in an increasingly diverse workforce; and thinking, studying, researching, and writing critically on what others have discovered can provide excitement, challenge, and serious work. Some accounting and business majors have loved this aspect of their academic work and want to continue that activity.

Others go on to graduate school for purely practical reasons; they have examined employment prospects in their field of study and all indications are that a graduate degree is required. If you have earned a B.S. in accounting as a stepping stone to a career in upper-level management or tax law, for example, going on for further training is mandatory. As a bachelor's level accounting major, you cannot move above the assistant level without a master's degree or in some cases a law degree. A review of jobs in different areas will suggest that at least a master's degree is important to be competitive.

Alumni who are working in the government, for public accounting firms, or for private corporations can tell you which degrees are required in different settings. Ask your college career office for some alumni names and give them a call. Prepare some questions on specific job prospects in their field at each degree level. A thorough examination of the marketplace and talking to employers and professors will give you a sense of the scope of employment for a bachelor's, master's, or other related degree.

College teaching will require an advanced degree. Accounting might demand specialization in an additional field, such as computers or law. The more senior executive positions in the career paths outlined in this book will require advanced education and perhaps a particular specialization in a subject area (finance, worker's comp, or taxation, for example).

CONSIDER YOUR MOTIVES

The answer to the question of "Why graduate school?" is a personal one for each applicant. Nevertheless, it is important to consider your motives carefully. Graduate school involves additional time out of the employment market, a high degree of critical evaluation, significant autonomy as you pursue your studies, and considerable financial expenditure. For some students in doctoral programs, there may be additional life choice issues, such as relationships, marriage, and parenthood that may present real challenges while in a program of study. You would be well-advised to consider the following questions as you think about your decision to continue your studies.

Are You Postponing Some Tough Decisions by Going to School?
Graduate school is not a place to go to avoid life's problems. There is intense competition for graduate school slots and for the fellowships, scholarships, and

financial aid available. This competition means extensive interviewing, resume submission, and essay writing that rivals corporate recruitment. Likewise, the graduate school process is a mentored one in which faculty stay aware of and involved in the academic progress of their students and continually challenge the quality of their work. Many graduate students are called upon to participate in teaching and professional writing and research as well.

In other words, this is no place to hide from the spotlight. Graduate students work very hard and much is demanded of them individually. If you elect to go to graduate school to avoid the stresses and strains of the "real world," you will find no safe place in higher academics. Vivid accounts, both fiction and nonfiction, have depicted quite accurately the personal and professional demands of graduate school work.

The selection of graduate studies as a career option should be a positive choice—something you *want* to do. It shouldn't be selected as an escape from other, less attractive or more challenging options, nor should it be selected as the option of last resort (i.e., "I can't do anything else; I'd better just stay in school"). If you're in some doubt about the strength of your reasoning about continuing in school, discuss the issues with a career counselor. Together you can clarify your reasoning, and you'll get some sound feedback on what you're about to undertake.

On the other hand, staying on in graduate school because of a particularly poor employment market and a lack of jobs at entry-level positions has proven to be an effective "stalling" strategy. If you can afford it, pursuing a graduate degree immediately after your undergraduate education gives you a year or two to "wait out" a difficult economic climate while at the same time acquiring a potentially valuable credential.

Have You Done Some Hands-On Reality Testing?

There are experiential options available to give some reality to your decision-making process about graduate school. Internships or work in the field can give you a good idea about employment demands, conditions, and atmosphere.

· ·

An M.B.A. is the frequent choice of accounting majors who hope to enhance their careers. Publications such as the *Wall Street Journal's Managing Your Career* newspapers often contain articles that continue the public discussions over the wisdom of the M.B.A. choice.

For accounting majors who want to take their education to a higher level in preparation for college teaching, some hands-on reality testing is vital. Begin with your college professors and ask them to talk to you about their own educational and career paths to their current teaching posts. They can also tell about the time they spend outside the classroom, whether in research activities or in departmental meetings dealing with faculty and budget concerns.

Even after hearing the experience of only one professor, you will have a stronger concept of the pace of the job, interaction with colleagues, subject matter, and pressure to do research and publish results. Talking to people and asking questions is invaluable as an exercise to help you better understand the objective of your graduate study.

For accounting majors especially, the opportunity to do this kind of reality testing is priceless. It helps to identify what your real-world skills are and how they can be put to use. Internships and co-op experiences speed that process up and prevent the frustrating and expensive investigation many graduates begin only after graduation.

Do You Need an Advanced Degree to Work in Your Field?

Certainly there are fields such as law, psychiatry, medicine, and college teaching that demand advanced degrees. Is the field of employment you're considering one that also puts a premium on an advanced degree? You may be surprised. Read the want ads in a number of major Sunday newspapers for positions you would enjoy. How many of those require an advanced degree?

Retailing, for example, has always put a premium on what people can do, rather than how much education they have had. Successful people in retailing come from all academic preparations. A Ph.D. in English may bring only prestige to the individual employed as a magazine researcher. It may not bring a more senior position or better pay. In fact, it may disqualify you for some jobs because an employer might believe you will be unhappy to be overqualified for a particular position. Or your motives in applying for the work may be misconstrued, and the employer might think you will only be working at this level until something better comes along. None of this may be true for you, but it comes about because you are working outside of the usual territory for that degree level.

When economic times are especially difficult, we tend to see stories featured about individuals with advanced degrees doing what is considered unsuitable work, such as the Ph.D. in English driving a cab or the Ph.D. in chemistry waiting tables. Actually, this is not particularly surprising when you consider that as your degree level advances, the job market narrows appreciably. At any one time, regardless of economic circumstances, there are only so many jobs for your particular level of expertise. If you cannot find employment for your advanced degree level, chances are you will be considered suspect for many other kinds of employment and may be forced into temporary work far removed from your original intention.

Before making an important decision such as graduate study, learn your options and carefully consider what you want to do with your advanced degree. Ask yourself whether it is reasonable to think you can achieve your goals. Will there be jobs when you graduate? Where will they be? What will they pay? How competitive will the market be at that time, based on current predictions?

If you're uncertain about the degree requirements for the fields you're interested in, you should check a publication such as the U.S. Department of Labor's *Occupational Outlook Handbook.* Each entry has a section on training and other qualifications that will indicate clearly what the minimum educational requirement is for employment, what degree is the standard, and what employment may be possible without the required credential.

For example, for physicists and astronomers, a doctoral degree in physics or a closely related field is essential. Certainly this is the degree of choice in academic institutions. However, the *Occupational Outlook Handbook* also indicates what kinds of employment may be available to individuals holding a master's or even a bachelor's degree in physics.

Have You Compared Your Expectations of What Graduate School Will Do for You with What It Has Done for Alumni of the Program You're Considering?

Most colleges and universities perform some kind of postgraduate survey of their students to ascertain where they are employed, what additional education they have received, and what levels of salary they are enjoying. Ask to see this information either from the university you are considering applying to or from your own alma mater, especially if it has a similar graduate program. Such surveys often reveal surprises about occupational decisions, salaries, and work satisfaction. This information may affect your decision.

The value of self-assessment (the process of examining and making decisions about your own hierarchy of values and goals) is especially important in this process of analyzing the desirability of possible career paths involving graduate education. Sometimes a job requiring advanced education seems to hold real promise but is disappointing in salary potential or numbers of opportunities available. Certainly, it is better to research this information before embarking on a program of graduate studies. It may not change your mind about your decision, but by becoming better informed about your choice, you become better prepared for your future.

Have You Talked with People in Your Field to Explore What You Might Be Doing After Graduate School?

In pursuing your undergraduate degree, you will have come into contact with many individuals trained in the field you are considering. You might also have the opportunity to attend professional conferences, workshops, seminars, and job fairs where you can expand your network of contacts. Talk to them all! Find out about their individual career paths, discuss your own plans and hopes, and get their feedback on the reality of your expectations, and heed their advice about your prospects. Each will have a unique tale to tell, and each will bring a different perspective on the current marketplace for the credentials you are seeking. Talking to enough people will make you an expert on what's out there.

Are You Excited by the Idea of Studying the Particular Field You Have in Mind?

This question may be the most important one of all. If you are going to spend several years in advanced study, perhaps engendering some debt or postponing some lifestyle decisions for an advanced degree, you simply ought to enjoy what you're doing. Examine your work in the discipline so far. Has it been fun? Have you found yourself exploring various paths of thought? Do you read in your area for fun? Do you enjoy talking about it, thinking about it, and sharing it with others? Advanced degrees often are the beginning of a lifetime's involvement with a particular subject. Choose carefully a field that will hold your interest and your enthusiasm.

It is fairly obvious by now that we think you should give some careful thought to your decision and take some action. If nothing else, do the following:

- Talk and question (remember to listen!)
- Reality-test
- Soul-search by yourself or with a person you trust

FINDING THE RIGHT PROGRAM FOR YOU: SOME CONSIDERATIONS

There are several important factors in coming to a sound decision about the right graduate program for you. You'll want to begin by locating institutions that offer appropriate programs, examining each of these programs and their requirements, undertaking the application process by obtaining catalogs and application materials, visiting campuses if possible, arranging for letters of recommendation, writing your application statement, and finally following up on your applications.

Locate Institutions with Appropriate Programs

Once you decide on a particular advanced degree, it's important to develop a list of schools offering such a degree program. Perhaps the best sources of graduate program information are Peterson's *Guides to Graduate Study.* Use these guides to build your list. In addition, you may want to consult the College Board's *Index of Majors and Graduate Degrees,* which will help you find graduate programs offering the degree you seek. It is indexed by academic major and then categorized by state.

Now, this may be a considerable list. You may want to narrow the choices down further by a number of criteria: tuition, availability of financial aid, public versus private institutions, U.S. versus international institutions, size of student body, size of faculty, application fee (this varies by school; most fall within the $10–$75 range), and geographic location. This is only a partial list; you will have your own important considerations. Perhaps you are an avid scuba diver and you find it unrealistic to think you could pursue graduate study for a number of years without being able to ocean dive from time to time. Good! That's a decision and it's honest. Now, how far from the ocean is too far, and what schools meet your other needs? In any case, and according to your own criteria, begin to build a reasonable list of graduate schools that you are willing to spend the time investigating.

Examine the Degree Programs and Their Requirements

Once you've determined the criteria by which you want to develop a list of graduate schools, you can begin to examine the degree program requirements, faculty composition, and institutional research orientation. Again, using a resource such as Peterson's *Guides to Graduate Study* can reveal an amazingly rich level of material by which to judge your possible selections.

In addition to degree programs and degree requirements, entries will include information about application fees, entrance test requirements, tuition, percentage of applicants accepted, numbers of applicants receiving financial aid, gender breakdown of students, numbers of full- and part-time faculty, and often gender breakdown of faculty as well. Numbers graduating in each program and research orientations of departments are also included in some entries. There is information on graduate housing, student services, and library, research, and computer facilities. A contact person, phone number, and address are also standard pieces of information in these listings. In addition to the standard entries, some schools pay an additional fee to place full-page, more detailed program descriptions. The location of such a display ad, if present, would be indicated at the end of the standard entry.

It can be helpful to draw up a chart and enter relevant information about each school you are considering in order to have a ready reference on points of information that are important to you.

Undertake the Application Process

The Catalog. Once you've decided on a selection of schools, send for catalogs and applications. It is important to note here that these materials might take many weeks to arrive. Consequently, if you need the materials quickly, it might be best to telephone and explain your situation to see whether the process can be speeded up for you. Also, check a local college or university library, which might have current and complete college catalogs in a microfiche collection. These microfiche copies can provide you with helpful information while you wait for your own copy of the graduate school catalog or bulletin to arrive.

When you receive your catalogs, give them a careful reading and make notes of issues you might want to discuss on the telephone or in a personal interview, if that's possible. Does the course selection have the depth you had hoped for? What is the ratio of faculty to the required number of courses for your degree? How often will you encounter the same faculty member as an instructor?

....

If you are interested in graduate work in accounting, consider the availability of colloquiums, directed research opportunities, and specialized seminars in addition to classic courses in accounting theory and organizational behavior.

....

If, for example, your program offers a practicum or off-campus experience, who arranges this? Does the graduate school select a site and place you there, or is it your responsibility? What are the professional affiliations of the faculty? Does the program merit any outside professional endorsement or accreditation?

Critically evaluate the catalogs of each of the programs you are considering. List any questions you have and ask current or former teachers and colleagues for their impressions as well.

The Application. Preview each application thoroughly to determine what you need to provide in the way of letters of recommendation, transcripts from undergraduate schools or any previous graduate work, and personal essays that may be required. Make a notation for each application of what you need to complete that document.

Additionally, you'll want to determine entrance testing requirements for each institution and immediately arrange to complete your test registration. For example, the Graduate Record Exam (GRE) and the Graduate Management Admission Test (GMAT) each have thee to four weeks between the last registration date and the test date. Your local college career office should be able to provide you with test registration booklets, sample test materials, information on test sites and dates, and independent test review materials that might be available commercially.

Visit the Campus If Possible

If time and finances allow, a visit, interview, and tour can help make your decision easier. You can develop a sense of the student body, meet some of the faculty, and hear up-to-date information on resources and the curriculum. You will have a brief opportunity to "try out" the surroundings to see if they fit your needs. After all, it will be home for a while. If a visit is not possible but you have questions, don't hesitate to call and speak with the dean of the graduate school. Most are more than happy to talk to candidates and want them to have the answers they seek. Graduate school admission is a very personal and individual process.

Arrange for Letters of Recommendation

This is also the time to begin to assemble a group of individuals who will support your candidacy as a graduate student by writing letters of recommendation or completing recommendation forms. Some schools will ask you to provide letters of recommendation to be included with your application or sent directly to the school by the recommender. Other graduate programs will provide a recommendation form that must be completed by the recommender. These graduate school forms vary greatly in the amount of space provided for a written recommendation. So that you can use letters as you need to, ask your recommenders to address their letters "To Whom It May Concern," unless one of your recommenders has a particular connection to one of your graduate schools or knows an official at the school.

Choose recommenders who can speak authoritatively about the criteria important to selection officials at your graduate school. In other words, choose recommenders who can write about your grasp of the literature in your field of study, your ability to write and speak effectively, your class performance, and your demonstrated interest in the field outside of class. Other characteristics that graduate schools are interested in assessing include your emotional maturity, leadership ability, breadth of general knowledge, intellectual ability, motivation, perseverance, and ability to engage in independent inquiry.

When requesting recommendations, it's especially helpful to put the request in writing. Explain your graduate school intentions and express some of your thoughts about graduate school and your appreciation for their support. Don't be shy about "prompting" your recommenders with some suggestions of what you would appreciate being included in their comments. Most recommenders will find this direction helpful and will want to produce a statement of support that you can both stand behind. Consequently, if your interaction with one recommender was especially focused on research projects, he or she might be best able to speak of those skills and your critical thinking ability. Another recommender may have good comments to make about your public presentation skills.

Give your recommenders plenty of lead time in which to complete your recommendation, and set a date by which they should respond. If they fail to meet your deadline, be prepared to make a polite call or visit to inquire if they need more information or if there is anything you can do to move the process along.

Whether or not you are providing a graduate school form or asking for an original letter to be mailed, be sure to provide an envelope and postage if the recommender must mail the form or letter directly to the graduate school.

Each recommendation you request should provide a different piece of information about you for the selection committee. It might be pleasant for letters of recommendation to say that you are a fine, upstanding individual, but a selection committee for graduate school will require specific information. Each recommender has had a unique relationship with you, and their letters should reflect that. Think of each letter as helping to build a more complete portrait of you as a potential graduate student.

Write Your Application Statement

• •

For the accounting major, the application and personal essay should be a welcome opportunity to express interest in pursuing graduate study. Your understanding of the challenges ahead, your commitment to the work involved, and your expressed self-awareness will weigh heavily in the decision process of the graduate school admissions committee.

• •

An excellent source to help in thinking about writing this essay is *How to Write a Winning Personal Statement for Graduate and Professional School* by Richard J. Stelzer. It has been written from the perspective of what graduate school selection committees are looking for when they read these essays. It provides helpful tips to keep your essay targeted on the kinds of issues and criteria that are important to selection committees and that provide them with the kind of information they can best utilize in making their decision.

Follow Up on Your Applications

After you have finished each application and mailed it along with your transcript requests and letters of recommendation, be sure to follow up on the progress of your file. For example, call the graduate school administrative staff to see whether your transcripts have arrived. If the school required your recommenders to fill out a specific recommendation form that had to be mailed directly to the school, you will want to ensure that they have all arrived in good time for the processing of your application. It is your responsibility to make certain that all required information is received by the institution.

RESEARCHING FINANCIAL AID SOURCES, SCHOLARSHIPS, AND FELLOWSHIPS

Financial aid information is available from each school, so be sure to request it when you call for a catalog and application materials. There will be several lengthy forms to complete, and these will vary by school, type of school (public versus private), and state. Be sure to note the deadline dates for these important forms.

There are many excellent resources available to help you explore all of your financial aid options. Visit your college career office or local public library to find out about the range of materials available. Two excellent resources include Peterson's *Grants for Graduate Students* and the Foundation Center's *Foundation Grants to Individuals*. These types of resources generally contain information that can be accessed by indexes including field of study, specific eligibility requirements, administering agency, and geographic focus.

EVALUATING ACCEPTANCE

If you apply to and are accepted at more than one school, it is time to return to your initial research and self-assessment to evaluate your options and select the program that will best help you achieve the goals you set for pursuing graduate study. You'll want to choose a program that will allow you to complete your studies in a timely and cost-effective way. This may be a good time to get additional feedback from professors and career professionals who are familiar with your interests and plans. Ultimately, the decision is yours, so be sure you get answers to all the questions you can think of.

SOME NOTES ABOUT REJECTION

Each graduate school is searching for applicants who appear to have the qualifications necessary to succeed in its program. Applications are evaluated on a combination of undergraduate grade point average, strength of letters of recommendation, standardized test scores, and personal statements written for the application.

A carelessly completed application is one reason many applicants are denied admission to a graduate program. To avoid this type of needless rejection, be sure to carefully and completely answer all appropriate questions on the application form, focus your personal statement given the instructions provided, and submit your materials well in advance of the deadline. Remember that your test scores and recommendations are considered a part of your application, so they must also be received by the deadline.

If you are rejected by a school that especially interests you, you may want to contact the dean of graduate studies to discuss the strengths and weaknesses of your application. Information provided by the dean will be useful in reapplying to the program or applying to other, similar programs.

PART TWO

THE CAREER PATHS

CHAPTER NINE

INTRODUCTION TO ACCOUNTING CAREER PATHS

*"The promises of yesterday are
the taxes of today."*

—William Lyon Mackenzie King

How can you best express your interest in accounting? Examine your skills, abilities, strengths, weaknesses, standards, priorities, goals, dreams, and hopes in order to determine which area of accounting is the best fit for you. Then ask yourself the following questions:

- Am I more attracted to public accounting, private accounting, government accounting, or accounting education?
- Do I want a 9 to 5 job, or do I not mind working longer hours—sometimes much longer hours?
- Do I mind traveling?
- Do I like the idea of being my own boss?
- Do I enjoy working with a limited number of people or with a larger number of people?
- Am I good at passing along information to others?
- Do I like to be in charge or do I prefer to have others in charge?
- Do I enjoy teaching?
- Do I have a specific area in accounting that particularly interests me?

❏ Do I prefer to work at home on my own or in an office setting?

Answering these questions will give you a starting point.

IN THIS BOOK

Though this book does not provide information about every career that would be possible for an accounting major, the chapters that follow offer a considerable amount of information about many careers in this field. The four career paths described in this book include:

1. Public accounting

2. Management accounting

3. Government accounting

4. Accounting education

Accounting is a wide field that provides many opportunities to those who are willing to prepare themselves and work hard to achieve success. Read on to determine which area of accounting appeals to you most, and then take the necessary steps to fulfill your dreams.

"Far and away the best prize that life offers is the chance to work hard at work worth doing."

—Theodore Roosevelt

CHAPTER TEN

PATH 1: PUBLIC ACCOUNTING

"Every good citizen ... should be willing to devote a brief time during some one day in the year, when necessary, to the making up of a listing of his income for taxes ... to contribute to his Government, not the scriptural tithe, but a small percentage of his net profits."

—Representative Cordell Hull (1913)

HELP WANTED

Public Accountant

Our company, one of Chicago's top 25 public accounting firms, has a team-oriented, client-focused environment encouraging creativity, initiative, and the free flow of ideas. Our diversified client base consists of highly successful, privately held companies in a variety of industries; nonprofit organizations; and individuals. An excellent opportunity exists for a bright, ambitious, entrepreneurial individual with good business sense. Strong theoretical background (with the ability to apply it) and outstanding interpersonal skills necessary. A bachelor's degree in accounting, CPA credentials, and recent public accounting experience are required. Please send resume.

All around the world, accounting is an integral part of every business. Once considered one of the quieter occupations, it has undergone a dramatic renaissance. Taxation and auditing are areas of great importance, and accountants have now entered nontraditional areas such as management consulting, litigation support, valuation, estate planning, and personal financial planning. The accounting profession now offers a wide variety of opportunities for all who decide to enter and put in the required amount of effort.

DEFINITION OF THE CAREER PATH

Public Accountant
Certified Public Accountant

Public accountants (PAs) and certified public accountants (CPAs), who either head their own businesses or work for accounting firms, provide a broad range of accounting, auditing, tax, and consulting services for their clients, who may be individuals, companies, corporations, governments, or nonprofit organizations. All accountants perform similar duties, but CPAs have additional credentials. (See "Training and Qualifications," page 116, for details.)

Within each field, accountants may choose from a number of specialties. For example, many public accountants concentrate on tax matters, such as preparing individual income tax returns and advising companies of the tax advantages and disadvantages of certain business decisions. Others concentrate on consulting and offer advice on matters such as employee health care benefits and compensation; the design of companies' accounting and data processing systems; and controls to safeguard assets. Some specialize in forensic accounting, investigating and interpreting bankruptcies and other complex financial transactions. Still others work primarily in auditing—examining a client's financial statements and reporting to investors and authorities that they have been prepared and reported correctly.

With the widespread use of computers, the amount of number crunching that accountants perform has been dramatically reduced. (Of course, it goes without saying that it is still important for a public accountant to have a solid understanding of numbers and financial concepts in order to do her job well.) Now, with the aid of special software packages, accountants summarize transactions in standard formats for financial records or organize data in special formats for financial analysis. These accounting packages greatly reduce the amount of tedious manual work associated with figures and records. Some packages require few specialized computer skills, while others require formal training. Personal and laptop computers enable accountants and auditors in all fields, even those who work independently, to use their clients' computer systems and to extract information from large mainframe computers.

In an accounting firm, meetings are a fact of life for all staff members. There are planning meetings, which are designed to create proposals to secure client business; proposal meetings, where staff pitch a proposal to the client; client meetings, where staff plan for the client; meetings for staff reviews; meetings to plan strategy for the firm; and meetings to receive continuing professional education. This adds up to a staggering number of meetings on a monthly basis.

There is also a great deal of writing that must be done, so it is important for accountants to have a good command of the English language and to be comfortable with writing. For instance, it is often important to record discussions with clients and advice given to them so that no confusion exists later. This must be done clearly and accurately. In the tax area, there are many research projects where both the problem that is being researched and the conclusions that are reached must be reduced to writing.

In a large accounting firm, the amount of interaction with people is much greater than one might expect. First, the number of the firm's staff involved in any given project can be quite large. Second, the client may have a number of people devoted to a project. Third, the accountant is usually involved with a large number of clients.

Since public accountants are free of special interest in one business or client, they can make fair, unbiased judgments. Often a person or business relies solely on a public accountant for advice on money management. Public accountants also give families advice on money and taxes. They prepare estate, gift, inheritance, and income tax statements. Public accountants work with lawyers and insurance and trust experts. Together they set up or carry out estate plans and take care of other money matters.

A CPA who has been with a firm five to seven years usually reaches a supervisory level. That person spends a large part of the time doing just that—supervising. He is responsible for getting returns out the door, keeping clients and partners happy, seeing to it that the staff is satisfied and busy, and making sure that projects get done both correctly and in a timely fashion.

POSSIBLE JOB TITLES

Accountant	External auditor
Accounting practitioner (AP)	Forensic accountant
Auditor	Public accountant (PA)

Certified public accountant (CPA)   Registered public accountant (RPA)

Consultant   Tax specialist

POSSIBLE EMPLOYERS

Accountants and auditors held about 962,000 jobs in 1994. They worked throughout private industry and government, but nearly one-third worked for accounting, auditing, and bookkeeping firms, or were self-employed. Recent figures reveal that there were 501,000 state-licensed certified public accountants (CPAs), public accountants (PAs), registered public accountants (RPAs), and accounting practitioners (APs).

Nearly every organization that has an income must have an accountant, either full- or part-time, to help keep track of money issues. Therefore, accountants may be employed by an individual, company, corporation, or nonprofit organization.

Most accountants and auditors work in urban areas where public accounting firms and central or regional offices of businesses are concentrated. The largest firms are called the "Big Six." They include:

Arthur Andersen & Company
33 West Monroe Street
Chicago, IL 60603

Coopers & Lybrand, LLP
1251 Avenue of the Americas
New York, NY 10020

Deloitte and Touche
10 Westport Road
P.O. Box 820
Wilton, CT 06897

Ernst & Young
277 Park Avenue
New York, NY 10172

KPMG Peat Marwick and Company
345 Park Avenue
New York, NY 10154

Price Waterhouse
1251 Avenue of the Americas
New York, NY 10020

RELATED OCCUPATIONS

Accountants and auditors analyze financial information and design internal control systems. Others for whom training in accounting is invaluable include appraisers, budget officers, tax preparers, bookkeepers, those working in bank services, loan officers, financial analysts and managers, bank officers, actuaries, underwriters, tax collectors, revenue agents, FBI special agents, securities sales representatives, and purchasing agents.

WORKING CONDITIONS

Accountants and auditors work in offices, but public accountants may frequently visit the offices of clients while conducting audits. Self-employed accountants may be able to do part of their work at home.

A large number of accountants and auditors generally work a standard 40-hour week, but many work longer, particularly if they are self-employed and free to take on the work of as many clients as they choose. For example, about 4 out of 10 self-employed accountants and auditors work more than 50 hours per week, compared to 1 out of 4 wage and salary accountants and auditors. Many accountants often work long hours during the tax season—January until April 15th.

The profession involves considerable contact with customers and the possibility of travel.

TRAINING AND QUALIFICATIONS

Persons planning a career in accounting should have an aptitude for mathematics; be able to analyze, compare, and interpret facts and figures quickly; and make sound judgments based upon this knowledge. They must be able to clearly communicate the results of their work, both orally and in writing. Accountants and auditors must be good at working with people as well as with business systems and computers. Desirable personal traits include neatness, patience, self-discipline, responsibility, and accuracy.

Most public accounting and business firms require applicants for accountant and auditor positions to have at least a bachelor's degree in accounting or a related field. Those wishing to pursue a bachelor's degree in accounting should carefully research accounting curricula before enrolling. Private business schools, junior colleges, and some technical schools also offer training programs. In these programs, students take courses in mathematics, accounting methods, and computers.

Previous experience in accounting or auditing can help an applicant get a job. Many colleges offer students an opportunity to gain experience through summer or part-time internship programs conducted by public accounting or business firms. Such training is advantageous in gaining permanent employment in the field.

Professional recognition through certification or licensing is also helpful. In most states, CPAs are the only accountants who are licensed and regulated. Anyone working as a CPA must have a certificate and a license issued by a state board of accountancy. The vast majority of states require CPA candidates to be college graduates, but a few states substitute a certain number of years of public accounting experience for the educational requirement. Based on recommendations made by the American Institute of Certified Public Accountants, a small number of states currently require that CPA candidates complete 150 semester hours of college coursework, but most states are working toward adopting this recommendation. (By January 1, 2001, at least 32 states will have this requirement.) The 150-hour rule requires an additional 30 hours of coursework beyond the usual four-year bachelor's degree in accounting. The composition of the additional 30 hours of coursework is unspecified by most states.

All states use the four-part Uniform CPA Examination prepared by the American Institute of Certified Public Accountants. The two-day CPA examination is rigorous, and only about one-quarter of those who take it each year pass each part they attempt. Candidates are not required to pass all four parts at once, although most states require candidates to pass at least two parts for partial credit. Many states require all sections of the test to be passed within a certain period of time. Most states also require applicants for a CPA certificate to have some accounting experience.

The designations PA or RPA are also recognized by most states, and several states continue to issue these licenses. With the growth in the number of CPAs, however, the majority of states are phasing out the PA, RPA, and other non-CPA designations by not issuing any more new licenses. Accountants who hold PA or RPA designations have similar legal rights, duties, and obligations as CPAs, but their qualifications for licensure are less stringent. The designation *accounting practitioner* is also awarded by several states. It requires less formal training than a CPA license and covers a more limited scope of practice.

Nearly all states require both CPAs and PAs to complete a certain number of hours of continuing professional education before their licenses can be renewed. The professional associations representing accountants sponsor numerous courses, seminars, group study programs, and other forms of continuing education.

Professional societies bestow other forms of credentials on a voluntary basis. Voluntary certification can attest to professional competence in a specialized field of accounting and auditing. It also can certify that a recognized level of professional competence has been achieved by accountants and auditors who acquired some skills on the job, without the amount of formal education or public accounting work experience needed to meet the rigorous standards required to take the CPA examination. Employers increasingly seek applicants with these credentials.

To stay current, most accountants study continuously.

EARNINGS

According to a salary survey conducted by the National Association of Colleges and Employers, candidates with a bachelor's degree in accounting received starting offers averaging $27,900 a year in 1995; those with a master's degree in accounting, $31,500.

According to a survey of workplaces in 160 metropolitan areas, accountants with limited experience had median earnings of $25,400 in 1993, with the middle half earning between $23,000 and $28,200. The most experienced accountants had median earnings of $77,200, with the middle half earning between $70,300 and $85,400. Public accountants employed by public accounting firms with limited experience had median earnings of $28,100 in 1993, with the middle half earning between $26,900 and $29,400. The most experienced public accountants had median earnings of $48,800, with the middle half earning between $41,300 and $54,400. However, many owners and partners of firms earned considerably more.

Most full-time accounting professionals usually receive benefits, including paid vacations, health and life insurance, and pension plans.

CAREER OUTLOOK

CPAs should continue to enjoy the widest range of job opportunities, especially as more states enact the 150-hour requirement, making it more difficult to become a CPA. Competition for the most prestigious jobs, such as those with major accounting and business firms, will remain keen. Applicants with a master's degree in accounting or a master's degree in business administration with a concentration in accounting are increasingly valued, particularly among large firms. As computers now perform many increasingly complex accounting functions and allow accountants and auditors to analyze more information, a broad base of computer experience is also advantageous. Expertise in specialized areas such as international business, specific industries, or current legislation may also be helpful in landing certain accounting and auditing jobs.

Employment of accountants and auditors is expected to grow about as fast as the average for all occupations through the year 2005. Although the profession is characterized by a relatively low rate of turnover, because the occupation is so large, the need to replace accountants and auditors who retire or move into other occupations will produce thousands of additional job openings annually.

As the economy grows, the number of business establishments increases, requiring more accountants and auditors to set up books, prepare taxes, and provide management advice. As these businesses grow, the volume and complexity of information developed by accountants and auditors on costs, expenditures, and taxes will increase as well. More complex requirements for accountants and auditors also arise from changes in legislation related to taxes, financial reporting standards, business investments, mergers, and other financial matters. In addition, businesses will increasingly need quick, accurate, and individually tailored financial information due to the demands of growing international competition.

The changing roles of public accountants, management accountants, and internal auditors also will spur job growth. Public accountants will perform less auditing work due to potential liability, and less tax work due to growing competition from tax preparation firms; but they will assume an even greater management advisory role and expand their consulting services. These rapidly growing services will lead to increased demand for public accountants in the coming years.

STRATEGY FOR FINDING THE JOBS

A large number of accountants are hired into CPA firms directly out of school. Many of the larger firms recruit on college and graduate school campuses. Candidates who have managed to gain some basic accounting work experience during college and have served at least one internship have an edge in the hiring process. They are perceived to have a better sense of the actual mechanics of accounting and have demonstrated their willingness to work even while pursuing their academic degrees.

Experts recommend that individuals decide on their area of specialty in the profession as soon as possible. This will allow you to develop your skills much more rapidly in the specialty you choose.

PROFESSIONAL ASSOCIATIONS

American Institute of Certified Public Accountants
Harborside Financial Center
Plaza III, Floors 2 and 3
Jersey City, NJ 07311-3881

American Society of Women Accountants
35 East Wacker Drive
Suite 1036
Chicago, IL 60601

American Women Society of Certified Public Accountants
401 North Michigan Avenue
Chicago, IL 60611-4267

National Association of Accountants
10 Paragon Drive
Montvale, NJ 07645

National Society of Public Accountants and the Accreditation Council for Accountancy and Taxation
1010 North Fairfax Street
Alexandria, VA 22314

MEET DEBRA SCHILL

Debra Schill earned a Bachelor of General Studies degree from Indiana University in Indianapolis, majoring in business/accounting. She is a CPA with an Indiana license, a self-employed CPA in public accounting, and a financial planner. She also owns a Triple Check business, which includes Triple Check Income Tax Services, Triple Check Financial Services, and Triple Check Business Services.

"I was attracted to the profession because I really enjoyed preparing taxes," she says. "Since that work was seasonal, I decided that I would also enjoy doing similar work year-round, so I changed my college major from computer science to accounting. While in college, I worked for several years in the banking industry, first as a teller, then as a bookkeeper, proof operator, and clerk in the trust department. At the same time,

continued

continued

I also worked part-time as a tax preparer for an H&R Block office. The tasks I enjoyed most in each of those jobs had to do with finances. I enjoyed handling money, was fascinated by the wealth I saw some individuals accumulate, and enjoyed watching how they managed it. I always like doing data entry work and filling out forms, and I had a good ability for solving problems. It seemed that by becoming an accountant and financial planner, I would be able to work with people in many areas, help them accumulate wealth, and manage that wealth through investment planning and wise tax planning.

"In September of 1994, I purchased an existing tax and book-keeping business. The company's workload varies according to the time of the year. During tax season (January through April), I work seven days a week, from 6 to 18 hours per day. The days are filled with appointments with clients to collect information for their tax returns. During tax season, evenings and weekends are dedicated to filling out those tax returns, getting them processed and out the door. During this time my office is hectic, with lots of people coming and going. During the rest of the year, my hours are usually from 9 to 5, with an occasional evening or weekend appointment. This is also a time when I concentrate on marketing plans to help my business grow and see clients for financial planning and tax planning, while managing the work schedules for two or more employees.

"I really enjoy working with people and helping them solve their financial problems. I can help them plan their financial futures and accomplish their goals. The downside for me would be the sales and marketing necessary to grow my business. I don't enjoy the sales responsibilities, which include cold-calling and making new contacts. I would rather have referrals of new business from my clients.

"You really need to care about people and want to help them," she stresses. "Many people can succeed financially in this business without caring, but clients really can sense when you care more for yourself than for them. Also, you need to have a lot of support from your family. The seasonal workload is so heavy that you work very long hours. More than one-half to two-thirds of your annual income is produced in a three-month period. Many spouses and children simply don't understand the commitment necessary, and it can cause problems."

MEET GERRI GREEN

Gerri Green earned a bachelor's degree in psychology at the University of Connecticut and her M.B.A. in accounting at the University of Hartford. She now serves as a CPA in the state of Connecticut. During her 22 years in the accounting field, she has been employed by a very small local CPA firm as a staff accountant; a huge insurance company; a Big Six CPA firm as tax supervisor; a Fortune 500 corporation as a United States tax manager; a medium-sized CPA firm; a family-owned business as a consultant; and a medium-sized CPA firm as a partner (first part-time, then full-time).

She is also a part-time freelance writer who has received the Distinguished Author Award from the Connecticut Society of CPAs, and has served as editor of an accounting journal and chair of the Connecticut Society of CPAs' publications committee.

"For the past eight years, I have also served as an adjunct accounting teacher and adviser for students at the college level," she says. "Several years ago, I seriously explored the possibility of getting my Ph.D. in accounting so I could teach full-time, research, and write. The first year I applied I was on the waiting list. The second year I could have gone, but I was made partner at the CPA firm I was with, so I decided against school.

"Several months ago, I left my position as partner of a CPA firm. I had joined that firm four years ago (after thoughtful reflection on all my other experiences) to work in a small-firm environment. It was wonderful until early this year, when the firm merged with two others to form the largest non-Big Six firm in the area. Since this change included a move into an office tower in the city, I made the decision to leave. My already long commute would have been even longer, and I wanted more flexibility with my time and my life than the new firm would have provided. Now I'm engaged in Internet training for CPAs and others and doing more writing. And I look forward to whatever is next!"

MEET LIANE MICHELE LEMONS

Liane Michele Lemons is a graduate of Boise State University in Boise, Idaho, having received her Bachelor of Arts degree

continued

continued

in accounting. Presently, she is the owner of her own tax practice—Liane M. Lemons, CPA—in Boise, Idaho.

"My first accounting job was in 1986 as an accounting intern for the Internal Revenue Service," she says. After graduating in 1987, I became a revenue agent (auditor) for the IRS.

"I always liked numbers and math," says Liane. "In 1982, while a junior in high school, I worked for someone I admired, a CPA who was the owner of a resort called Hidden Paradise. The business teacher at my high school was also a CPA, and both acted as positive role models who lead me into accounting. I had never really done accounting before that, but once I decided what I wanted to do, I never looked back.

"Since I am a small-business owner who focuses on small businesses, my work atmosphere is very casual. We don't frequently dress up or even have a strict dress code. The work is very hectic. A typical day would include bookkeeping, speaking with the IRS, preparing reports, doing taxes, and meeting with clients. No two days are ever the same, nor are any two clients. I take a personal interest in my clients, so I have the opportunity to meet many interesting people.

"I typically work 40 to 50 hours a week during the off season, and from 9 A.M. until midnight during tax season. Demands change on a daily basis, and stress is very high for me on most days. I spend a lot of time responding to problems and putting out fires. I find that I have to take time off to keep from burning out. I spend almost all day in front of a computer, and have become a lot more computer literate that I ever imagined I would be. Since I engage in both tax work and accounting, I constantly face looming deadlines, which adds to the pressure of the day. However, I do enjoy my work, and feel I am very good at it. In fact, I was named the Region X Accountant Advocate of the Year by the United States Small Business Administration.

"I am happy that I have the ability to meet and observe a variety of people in vastly different economic and social circumstances. I also get to know and understand a lot of different businesses and industries intimately, which is very rewarding both to me and my clients. I truly enjoy seeing the work I do help people succeed. The thing that I like least is having to be at clients' beck and call. Some people act as if

continued

continued

they are the only client I have, and expect to be given top priority every time they call. It is also frustrating to deal with people who don't listen and then end up in trouble as a result of ignoring my advice.

"In my opinion, accounting is a great profession to go into, with a lot of potential for growth and expansion, and I think it is a career field that will continue to support people well into the future. I would encourage anyone to spend some time working with the IRS, a Big Six accounting firm, or even a larger regional firm to get strong experience and learn the ropes. If someone has the intention of going out on their own, I would probably recommend that they start with a smaller firm so they can get the experience they need to work with clients and understand the management end of the business. This business involves a lot of repetition, so if one is bothered by that, it would be a poor professional choice. The biggest key is taking the time to understand accounting and to get the necessary experience."

MEET THOMAS R. HILEMAN

Thomas R. Hileman received his Bachelor of Science degree from Penn State University in 1972. He now serves as president/shareholder of Hileman and Associates, PC.

"I started in accounting in 1972 after graduation," he says. "In 1973, I began to do public accounting and realized I loved it. No two problems were the same and I got to work with a lot of people. Since I am a people person, that was a plus. I struck out on my own in 1983 and have never looked back. I was attracted to the freedoms it provided for me. If you are successful in public accounting, you can pick and choose your clients. I am very happy to say that most of my clients are now good friends.

"Because of the nature of my practice, I spend a large portion of my day on the phone with clients trying to solve their problems. If the client is big enough, they might have someone on staff to handle some of what I do; although one of my

continued

continued

clients is a $40-million-a-year concern, and I function almost as its chief financial officer (CFO). No major financial decisions are made without my involvement.

"My office has a friendly, almost homey atmosphere. Because we have to put in long hours on various special projects such as litigation support, we are pretty laid back most of the time. In fact, on Fridays everyone can dress in business casual.

"I really enjoy the people, the mental challenges, and the fact that I am financially rewarded for my efforts. What I like least are the hours and having to always be in the client acquisition mode.

"I would recommend that those interested in this field work for a firm with good technical capabilities. Try to work in as many areas as possible. In other words, don't just do tax work or strictly audit work. You need as great a variety of background to draw on as possible."

MEET SHERRY L. McCOY

Sherry L. McCoy earned dual Bachelor of Science degrees in business from Eastern Illinois University—one in accounting and one in finance. Landing a position with McGladrey and Pullen, LLP in Peoria, Illinois, in June 1990 through campus recruiting, she now serves as general services manager for their branch in Pasadena, California.

"Though I can't pinpoint the moment, and while I am still an avid animal lover, somewhere between sixth grade and seventh grade my career interest switched from veterinarian to accountant," she says. "In part, I credit my uncle, who is a CPA, for this. Though we never really talked much about his work, I'm sure that's where I first heard the term *certified public accountant.*

"During my freshman or sophomore year in high school, I did a career research paper on accounting, learning that in England, CPAs are called 'chartered accountants.' The rest, as they say, is history. My first (and only) accounting class in high school was the perfect preparation for college. The teacher and I bonded perfectly. Without a doubt, that course was the

continued

continued

foundation for my perfect test scores in my first college accounting course!

"I could mention many professors and administrators at Eastern Illinois University, throughout the business department and other disciplines, who played a key role in those formative years. However, for brevity, I will simply say that we are all a product of our past, and I am deeply thankful for those whose paths I crossed. And to my parents, who never put barriers on my own testing and stretching of abilities, eternal thanks!

"My degrees are in accounting and finance, and while I was relatively certain of accounting as a career, I had an interest in finance courses due to the practical nature of information such as banking, insurance, real estate—all are things we need for daily living from a financial perspective.

"I did work for Ford Motor Credit Company during two summers of my college career. The staff there was great, but I knew I didn't want to spend the first few years of my professional career making credit collection calls. So I focused on accounting, particularly public accounting, since it seemed to offer the greatest exposure to a variety of people and industries.

"Like the saying goes, the only constant in change is constant change. So it is with my days. Of course, there is always a general scheme of events, but many days are spent simply being flexible when it comes to specifics. Likewise, some days are unbelievably busy while others proceed at a much more manageable rate (and on most days, I don't know which will occur).

"I wish I could outline a typical day—but there's really no such thing, in my opinion, unless you want to be extremely general in the discussion. In that case, most days begin with a cup of coffee and a review of the day's calendar while checking voice mail and E-mail for new messages. From there, days are spent in the office or at a client location (with many days including a bit of both). My present responsibilities basically focus on client service in the area of financial and compliance auditing, with general business advice also included, and staff training. The public accounting industry is heavily reliant on on-the-job training. Thus, in most cases, I fulfill both of these responsibilities concurrently. In an environment where efficiency is highly regarded, this is especially important and rewarding as well.

continued

continued

"In terms of hours, the typical schedule is heaviest from October to March, especially concentrated in the January to March period due to year-end financial statements and related tax filing engagements. After April 15, my hours are ideally in the 40-hour-per-week range, while the 'busy season' times can hit 75 to 80 hours a week. Fortunately for me, the latter types of weeks have been minimal in my career.

"I have been fortunate to have excellent colleagues in the firm—both advisers and advisees. A variety of individuals have taken time to train me, and I certainly do my best to do the same, which is easy when you have a staff of people who are willing and able to learn and grow. Similarly, working with clients, no matter what the role, has been both challenging and rewarding, just more proof that life is really all about people!

"What I like most about public accounting at McGladrey and Pullen, LLP, is the variety: people, industries, job details, new ideas. I really can't imagine another job in which I could have the same variety of experiences, from walking into bank vaults for surprise cash counts to being forklifted to count Jacuzzis in a home improvement warehouse.

"The downside can sometimes also be variety—too many different directions to go and only one of me to get everything done. But the upside definitely surpasses those moments. If it weren't so, I would not continue in this line of work.

"I would advise others who are interested in entering this career to be prepared to take quick turns and frequent leaps, sometimes without seeing where you'll land! Most of all, look at each day as an adventure, learning from each opportunity and sharing a smile with someone else. After all, life is much too short to spend a day any other way!"

MEET GEORGE V. MARINO

George V. Marino holds a Bachelor of Business Administration degree from Pace University and a Master of science degree in taxation from Baruch College. He is the director of health-care services for Friedman, Alpren and Green, LLP, in New York.

continued

continued

He concentrates his practice exclusively in the healthcare field, providing consulting and accounting services to medical groups, Mobile Office Systems (MOSS), Independent Practice Associations (IPAs), and hospitals. With over 15 years of experience, he is responsible for growing and directing the firm's Healthcare Services Group. Most recently, he was responsible for developing the financial healthcare services for a New York regional accounting firm. While there, he pioneered the implementation of an industry-recognized standard physician practice management consulting program. A frequent lecturer and publisher, he serves on the board of Unicare, Inc. and Richmond Home Need Services, Inc. Additionally, he served as an administrative director for The Center for Research in Ambulatory Care Physician Profiling Project; currently serves as a government relations director for the New York State Society of Certified Public Accountants; and sits on the technical advisory committee of the CPA Healthcare Network. He is a member of the Medical Group Management Associate, Healthcare Financial Management Associate, Professional Association of Healthcare Office Managers, the National Health Lawyers Association, and the American Institute of CPAs.

"A CPA background allows for an understanding of finances, management, information systems, and marketing," he says. "The work is very diversified. I typically work on client projects in healthcare—financial consulting, developing new business opportunities for the firm, lecturing, and writing articles in my field. I enjoy interaction with other CPAs in my firm, developing client relationships, and consulting with new clients.

"The healthcare field is very rewarding, especially with the continuous changes due to managed care."

MEET M. L. JOSETTE HEWITT

M. L. Josette Hewitt earned a Bachelor of Science degree in commerce with a major in accounting, graduating cum laude. She has a diploma in industrial relations, and is a certified financial planner with security licenses in life, fire and casualty,

continued

continued

disability, and health insurance. She is an enrolled agent, certified financial planner, registered representative, insurance broker, and business consultant. After spending 10 years as a CPA in the Philippines, she came to the United States and began working as a tax preparer. In 1990, she became a Triple Check Income Tax Services licensee. Recently she branched out from the traditional accounting/tax consulting business to become a licensee of both Triple Check Financial Services and Triple Check Business Services as well.

"I had a desire to assist individuals and small-business owners in organizing their tax, bookkeeping, and financial status," she says. "Other than during income tax season, we have a very flexible time schedule to meet with our clients in a relaxed and comfortable manner. I like clients who are organized and up-to-date and who provide us with complete and current records and documents. I also appreciate those who realize the hard work that we do. I dislike clients who want us to do a lot of work but do not have the finances to pay our fees.

"I would advise others who are interested in this field to always be aggressive and to maintain a good attitude toward people."

MEET FREDERICK R. BERK

Frederick R. Berk received his Bachelor of Science degree in accounting from the State University of New York at Binghamton and obtained his CPA license in 1984. He is a partner in Friedman, Alpren and Green, LLP, where he serves in the real estate group. With extensive knowledge in real estate taxation, accounting, and auditing, he has participated in construction and development activities, income taxation, restructuring, and consulting. Recently, he has become involved with consulting and tax planning regarding passive losses, cancellation of indebtedness, real estate professional regulations, and the formation of real estate investment trusts. Additionally, he represents numerous institutions in loan restructuring and property cash flow analysis, which is utilized to determine the money due to the institutions. He has also

continued

continued

authored several real estate articles and is a member of the American Institute of Certified Public Accountants, the New York State Society of Certified Public Accounts (where he serves as a member on the real estate committee), and the National Realty Club. He is also treasurer of the Young Mortgage Bankers Association.

"I took an accounting course in high school, which I enjoyed," he says. "I was intrigued with the fact that someone could become a partner in an accounting firm with 8 to 12 years of experience. I worked on numerous jobs while in high school and college, and decided that this profession would provide me with a desirable path to success.

"I started in the accounting field in 1981 after college graduation," he says. "Though I received job offers from the Big Six, I decided that I would rather work for a smaller firm. At the time, Friedman, Alpren and Green, LLP, employed approximately 40 people. (Today we work with 115 people.)

"In a service business with numerous clients (or, as I refer to them, my bosses) all demanding expedient high-quality service, the day is extremely busy and sometimes hectic. Work hours vary from 35 to 75 hours per week. It is an atmosphere where people are professional and courteous.

"I enjoy working with numerous clients and being involved in several different engagements at a time. I also enjoy interacting with our staff. However, I would like to be able to spend more time with my family.

"In my profession, it is extremely important to be technically proficient and to gain the respect of your clients. I would advise others to spend time on developing networks that will enable them to obtain new business. The technically competent people will do well; however, the person who has a balance between technical ability and business promotion skills will be more successful."

MEET JOHN R. BAKER

John R. Baker earned a Bachelor of Science degree in accounting from Rockhurst College in Kansas City, Missouri.

continued

continued

He is president of Troupe, Kehoe, Whiteaker & Kent, LLC, in Kansas City, Missouri; a licensed CPA in the states of Missouri and Kansas; and a member of the Missouri Society of Certified Public Accountants and the American Institute of Certified Public Accountants.

"Accounting has interested me since I was in high school," he says. "So when I entered college I made it my major. Over the years, I have grown with the practice. (This firm is a third-generation firm.) Also, over the years I have worked my way up from junior accountant, to junior auditor, to individual in charge of audits, to manager, to partner.

"The work atmosphere is pretty relaxed. We are family oriented, with plenty of flexibility. Everyone is a professional, so each person does what it takes to get the job done. We maintain an open-door policy and are here to listen to our employees. Because of this, there isn't a division among staff. We expect everyone to do a quality job and get the job done.

"I like the people contact best, particularly the one-to-one time spent with clients. Anyone can crunch numbers or be technically competent, but working with people makes this job interesting. I least like having to account for every quarter-hour of my time.

"There is no typical day. I usually arrive at the office at 7:45 A.M. and leave around 6:00 P.M., putting in about 55 to 60 hours per week. I have a certain number of appointments, but things are constantly changing. It's like a moving target all the time. On average, 35 percent of my time is spent on administration and about 25 percent reviewing the work of other staff members. The remainder of my time is spent on daily duties, management issues, and special projects for clients. Our busiest season is January through April, and summer can also be quite strenuous.

"I think you need the following attributes to be successful in this field: flexibility; good communication skills; the ability to get clients to listen to you in a nondemanding way; the techniques necessary to work well with a variety of people; accounting skills; respect for what others do; and skills in marketing and networking.

"I would advise those interested in getting into this field to definitely educate themselves. It's important to attend school and major in accounting. You have to like the courses you

continued

continued

take—there has to be certain joy. If you don't feel it, you'll be miserable working as an accountant. Accounting is no longer an occupation where you sit in a corner. It includes marketing and working closely with people. You also need to have excellent computer skills. I'd pick the same field, if I had to do it over again. It's a good occupation, and is very strong for women right now."

MEET STUART KESSLER

Stuart Kessler earned a Bachelor of Arts degree from Brooklyn College, an M.B.A. from City College of New York, a Juris Doctor from Brooklyn Law School, and a Master of Laws (L.L.M.) degree in taxation from New York University. He has earned the Personal Financial Planning Specialist designation, was elected chair of the American Institute of Certified Public Accountants, and is past president of the New York State Society of Certified Public Accountants. He is now a partner in the accounting firm of Goldstein, Golub, and Kessler.

"I was attracted to the profession by a close friend, an accounting professor at Brooklyn College," he says. "Ironically, this professor taught Stanley Goldstein, Gerry Golub, and me (the three partners in the group), all at different times.

"Accounting is a people-oriented profession," he says. "To me, the prospect of joining the accounting profession was attractive because of the ease of going from client to client and to different offices. I liked the idea of being in a position to meet new people all the time.

"An average day includes a large number of meetings, phone calls, E-mails, and voice mails. The communications technology is very different now than it was when I began in this profession," he stresses.

"I meet with a number of clients every day on personal financial planning and tax issues," he says. "Some meetings are prospect or client lunches and there are also evening professional and social activities like tennis. Also, a considerable amount of time is spent in fulfilling professional obligations, such as for the AICPA.

continued

continued

"The atmosphere is professional, friendly, diligent, and conducive to learning. The hours can be long when you have many meetings and client appointments out of the office on a given day.

"What I enjoy most is the personal aspect of the job—dealing with clients and their families. I enjoy meeting and working with a lot of good people, many of whom I have made long-term friends (some for 30 to 45 years). To some degree, a CPA is closer to her client than any other professional, including a psychiatrist.

"What I like least are internal meetings (not involving clients), and billing and collection. It's also quite a challenge to keep up with the constant changes in law, especially tax law. There is a constant need to be on the leading edge, which requires a lot of outside reading.

"I would advise those interested in this field to take as many courses in liberal arts as possible, specifically writing, speech rhetoric, and reading comprehension."

MEET SUSAN WILT

Susan Wilt earned a Bachelor of Science degree in accounting from the University of Kansas, Lawrence, Kansas. She is presently employed by Arthur Andersen in Kansas City, Missouri, as a financial analyst.

"I have a strong math aptitude and knew I wanted to be an accountant after my first accounting class in college," she says. "I began working for Arthur Andersen right out of college.

"There is a tremendous amount of paperwork, analytical analysis, and customer service in this field. It's busy approximately 50 hours per week, but it's a good atmosphere.

"I enjoy the problem solving. Resolution is very rewarding to me. However, there is never a day that you really feel as if you are done. And the competition is perpetual.

"I would tell others to make sure you like working with numbers, reporting, and the profession in general because I can guarantee you that you'll have some very long days ahead of you."

MEET ALAN P. SKLAR

Alan P. Sklar earned a Bachelor of Science and Bachelor of Arts (B.S.B.A.) degree from Northwestern University, Evanston, Illinois, in 1960. He is a licensed CPA in Illinois and a senior partner with Gleeson, Sklar, Sawyers and Cumpata, LLP, in Skokie, Illinois. He has had experience with both a national and a local CPA firm.

"I liked math and thought that accounting was all math," he says. "I was wrong about that but I still ventured into the right profession.

"I founded this firm in 1967 (upon leaving the firm I was at after being offered a partnership) because I thought I could be more successful and have more control over the future on my own. Because we brought bright people into the firm, we now are a second-generation firm with over 80 people.

"My job is made up of three major areas: managing people and jobs; acting as a consultant in many areas; and business development. A typical day might include a breakfast, lunch, or even golf with contacts (brokers or lawyers) or clients. It could include conferences with the managers regarding the status of client engagements. It also could include telephone conferences or face-to-face meetings and consulting with clients.

"I like working with clients the most. It's very rewarding when you have helped a client's business.

"For someone wanting a career in public accounting today, I would recommend taking as many courses as you can in various aspects of communication, including writing and interpersonal skills. Also, within the five-year experience level, I think you should develop a specific consulting skill. For this developing skill, you will need additional education—for example, a master's degree in something like production or technology."

MEET GEORGE SIMPSON

George Simpson earned a Bachelor of Science degree from California State University at Los Angeles in 1965 with an accounting emphasis. He received his California CPA certificate in 1973 and his financial planning specialist designation from

continued

continued

AICPA in 1992. He is chief executive officer of GWS—a large tax preparation, financial service, and business service office located in southern California. He is affiliated with Triple Check Income Tax Services.

"I started preparing taxes in 1969 while working at Lockheed Aircraft. When one of my co-workers who prepared taxes part-time became ill, he asked me to help him out. In 1971, I started working for a CPA doing taxes full-time, and have been preparing taxes ever since.

"I love the challenge tax preparation offers. I enjoy helping others achieve their goals and prepare for their futures. I love to be creative in the interpretation of the tax laws.

"I was the accountant for my father's business while in high school and college. I then worked in the financial arena prior to working for the CPA in 1971.

"My job is stressful. I have eight employees that I have to challenge and direct. I have over 1,200 personal tax clients, plus an additional 1,400 in the office. During tax season I work from 8 A.M. to 11 P.M. Monday to Friday, 8 A.M. until 6 P.M. on Saturday, and noon to 6 P.M. on Sunday every week. The remaining weeks I work from 8 A.M. until 6 P.M. Monday to Friday. I spend my days preparing taxes, providing financial advice, and being available to staff. The atmosphere is congenial and enjoyable.

"To succeed in this field, I feel that you need good work ethics, the ability to get along with people, strong sales techniques, a good mind, and a positive attitude.

"There is very little I can say that is negative. Employee problems are sometimes stressful and tax season has many hours without a break, but it is what I live for. I've never regretted what I do for a living for a single day."

CHAPTER ELEVEN

PATH 2: MANAGEMENT ACCOUNTING

"Taxes, after all, are the dues that we pay for the privileges of membership in an organized society."

—Franklin D. Roosevelt

HELP WANTED

Accountant

The world's largest trading center for limited-edition collector's bells and one of the most successful marketers of collectible items is seeking accounting professionals to join our team. You'll work in our financial area, which handles the corporate accounting functions as well as financial analysis and reporting. You will be responsible for accounting, financial control and financial reporting, and analysis for a business unit. This position will focus on working with the marketing team to analyze activity as well as handle cash management. The qualified applicant must possess a B.A., accounting preferred, as well as a minimum of two years' experience with financial statement preparation and analysis. Computer proficiency a must and previous mainframe responsibility a plus. We're looking for a self-starter with good communication skills who can effectively manage multiple priorities simultaneously. We offer a competitive salary and comprehensive benefits package. Please forward your resume and salary history to us.

Management accountants comprise the largest group of accounting professionals. They are employed by industry or business firms to provide advice and make decisions related to financial investment, budgeting, forecasting, and other business operations. Often, they work under the direction of corporate controllers and, in turn, supervise a staff of accounting personnel.

DEFINITION OF THE CAREER PATH

Management accountants are also often called industrial, corporate, or private accountants. In their capacity as accounting professionals, they record and analyze the financial information of the companies for which they work. They also are responsible for performance evaluation, cost management, and asset management. They may be part of executive teams that are involved in strategic planning or new product development.

Management accountants analyze and interpret the financial information corporate executives need to make sound business decisions. They also prepare financial reports for nonmanagement groups, including stockholders, creditors, regulatory agencies, and tax authorities. Within accounting departments, they may work in financial analysis, planning and budgeting, cost accounting, and other areas.

From the start, management accountants must demonstrate their basic accounting techniques and ability to handle assignments. Mastering the various functions of their departments and understanding their department's place in the accounting structure are vital. At first, preparing reports and other work will be done under the eyes of senior accountants. As one gains experience, additional responsibilities are added. At the entry level, typical tasks include bookkeeping, writing and recording checks, filling out tax returns, and keeping files. After establishing competence, more advanced projects such as offering ideas on improved accounting procedures, financial planning, and preparing reports on company finances will be assigned.

Beginning management accountants often start as cost accountants, junior internal auditors, or trainees for other accounting positions. As they rise through the organization, they may advance to accounting manager, chief cost accountant, budget director, or manager of internal auditing. Some become controllers, treasurers, financial vice presidents, chief financial officers, or corporation presidents. Many senior corporation executives have a background in accounting, internal auditing, or finance.

The general accounting department handles daily business needs, such as payroll, budgeting, accounts receivable, accounts payable, general ledger, and financial statements. Accountants must pay close attention to all laws and regulations affecting daily business operations. They may also offer advice on affordability of purchases and services. In smaller firms, the title *general accountant* might be held by the individual who handles or directs most or all accounting functions. This individual would, in turn, work most closely with public accountants if the organization employs them.

Organizations engage independent CPAs to serve as management accountants providing assistance on such matters as:

❑ Setting up a reporting system for better control and decision making

❑ Improving production control procedures

❑ Installing a computer or costing accounting system

❑ Implementing a work measurement program designed to improve efficiency

In certain instances, businesses employ public accountants to conduct audits. In other situations, organizations divide their accounting needs between public and management accountants, giving some functions (such as taxes) to an outside firm and assigning day-to-day jobs (such as payroll and budgeting) to the internal staff. For this reason, the career paths and duties of management accountants vary considerably.

The following include some of the specialties followed by professionals in this field.

Management Consultant

Management consultants work in cost accounting, planning and budgeting, financial analysis, and other activities They take part in problem-solving and decision-making processes in business. They help set prices, manage cash, and obtain credit. Management consultants also prepare financial reports for stockholders, creditors, regulatory agencies, and tax authorities.

Tax Accountant

Tax accountants specialize in preparing and filing federal, state, and local tax returns and must be extremely knowledgeable about federal, state, and local tax laws. They examine accounts, records, and computer tax returns according to government regulations. They also may originate, revise, and install tax record systems, conduct research to determine the effects of taxes pertaining to business operations or decisions, and recommend alternate methods of operations to reduce tax liabilities. In a large number of cases, tax accountants have prior experience in public or government accounting.

Cost Accountant

Cost accountants determine the cost of operating a firm and are responsible for installing cost control procedures, supervising cost systems and methods, and compiling periodic reports of operating costs. Working with marketing and manufacturing departments, they devise cost analyses of labor, materials, and overhead, which are involved in determining operating budgets, prices of products, profits, contract adjustments, and development of new products. Their work is needed by manufacturing and service industries alike.

Budget Accountant

Budget accountants prepare budgets showing past and projected operating expenses, income, and profits; analyze the availability and effect of spending funds for capital investments (plant, equipment, and long-term product expenditures) and forecast the company's future cash flow. They prepare reports of their findings, which are used as a basis for management planning and decisions.

Systems Accountant

Systems accountants design, install, and review accounting systems and procedures. They determine which records and reports are necessary, examine current accounting methods, develop procedures for obtaining the needed information, and implement accounting systems that will accomplish the desired objectives. Their goals may be to produce more efficient and accurate accounting procedures, inventory controls, production records, sales forecasts, tax reports, and other vital business information. Because most companies use computers for their accounting systems, systems accountants must be knowledgeable of data processing methods and capable of operating such systems.

Internal Auditor

Internal auditing is a specialized area of management accounting that has attracted a great deal of interest in recent years. Because of the growing body of federal legislation concerning business accounting standards and public access to information about corporate finances, internal auditing has changed from the luxury it once was to an absolute necessity. The internal auditor conducts an independent appraisal from within the organization by analyzing, criticizing, and recommending improvements to internal financial practices. The internal auditor also ensures the safety and profitability of investments and assets, and seeks to uncover sources of waste and inefficiency.

By virtue of being inside the organization, the internal auditor is privy to confidential information that is not shared with auditing public accountants.

In addition to being a skilled accountant, the internal auditor must have a comprehensive understanding of all fundamental business areas: marketing, manufacturing, advertising, and stockholder relations. Internal auditing is an excellent path to an executive position. However, despite the thrill of investigation, internal auditing is largely a job of long hours and repetitive work. One must be an individual of exceptional diligence and concentration to do this type of work.

Internal auditors may recommend controls for their organization's computer system to ensure the reliability of the system and the integrity of the data. A growing number of accountants and auditors have extensive computer skills and specialize in correcting problems with software or developing software to meet unique data needs.

Internal auditors conduct operational audits, regulatory reviews, and other special projects. They look into operations such as research and development, production, personnel, marketing, and information systems. They recommend methods to increase efficiency, effectiveness, and profits.

In conducting an audit, internal auditors follow generally accepted auditing standards. They use sampling techniques to test the accuracy of transactions, the accounting system, and management information systems. They test the recorded amounts of inventories, property, and equipment. They compare orders and receipts with company records to confirm that transactions actually took place.

In evaluating the results of these inquiries, auditors apply their own judgment and experience. If questions arise, they expand the search to get further information. They satisfy themselves that the data on the books is accurate.

Internal auditors check inventories and audit payrolls. They look to see whether storage methods prevent theft or spoilage. Auditors may suggest a way to save energy and at the same time use by-products. They see whether the firm is meeting its schedules. They may make suggestions to clear up a bottleneck. They are also alert to the possibilities of fraud or theft. Reviewing and reporting to management about taxes, sales, purchasing, and advertising, internal auditors challenge the value of accounts receivable and look for unrecorded accounts payable. They are always looking for ways to improve productivity and cut costs.

Controller

The controller is the executive in charge of all accounting functions and summarized financial information for executive personnel. This individual must have a keen understanding of all business operations and the judgment to make sound financial planning decisions.

Treasurer

The treasurer handles the cash flow and all financial reserves and is involved with loans, credit, and investments. Many firms combine the functions of controller and treasurer into one position.

Chief Financial Officer

The chief financial officer oversees the controller, treasurer, chief internal auditor, and the accounting staff. He or she advises top executives as to the financial needs and stability of the organization.

HELP WANTED

Staff Accountant
Downtown firm seeks individual for general accounting responsibilities. Successful candidate will be an energetic self-starter with a B.A. in accounting, computer skills, and analytical skills who learns quickly and works independently. Primary duties include accounts payable, accounts receivable, journal entries, bank reconciliations, and account analysis. This service firm has a growing residential real estate portfolio of apartment buildings. Salary low- to mid-20s. Forward resume with salary history.

POSSIBLE JOB TITLES

Accountant	General accountant
Accounting manager	Industrial accountant
Auditor	Internal auditor
Budget accountant	Junior internal auditor
Budget director	Management accountant
Certified management accountant	Management consultant

Certified public accountant (CPA)	Manager of accounting
Chief cost accountant	Manager of internal auditing
Chief financial officer	Private accountant
Chief internal auditor	Senior accountant
Controller	Staff accountant
Corporate accountant	Systems accountant
Corporation president	Tax accountant
Cost accountant	Treasurer
Financial vice president	

HELP WANTED

Senior Staff Accountant

We are a premier manufacturer of quality office products. We seek a detail-oriented professional for our fast-paced finance department. The selected candidate will be responsible for the preparation and communication of consolidated financial statements, consolidated annual budget, and periodic consolidation forecasts. In addition, he will be involved with corporate LAN administration. This individual will be a degreed accountant with three years of experience, preferably in a manufacturing operating environment, who possesses the ability to communicate effectively. Computer proficiency a must. Public accounting background and CPA preferred. Business planning experience desired. We offer excellent salary and benefits. Send resume with salary history.

POSSIBLE EMPLOYERS

Management accountants may be hired by private businesses, nonprofit organizations, or industries, and may find work in any part of the United States. Most are employed in urban areas where accounting firms and the headquarters of businesses are located. More than 20 percent work in Washington, Los Angeles, Chicago, and New York.

The Institute of Internal Auditors reports that 100,000 or more internal auditors now work in the United States. Twenty thousand of them are employed in financial institutions. Firms with more than a thousand employees usually have their own internal auditors.

HELP WANTED

Senior Accountant
The selected candidate will develop monthly, quarterly, and annual financial reports; assist with the preparation and analysis of statutory reporting requirements; audit the flow of statistical data from source documents through input to resultant output; write and update data retrieval programs; and write comprehensive status reports. The position requires strong deadline/time management and teamwork abilities. A B.S./B.A. in accounting or finance, more than three years' experience in accounting or finance, and experience with Excel, Word, and/or Access are essential. Insurance experience and/or a CPA is a plus. Applicants must be able to work extra hours as needed.

RELATED OCCUPATIONS

The Employment and Training Administration of the United States Department of Labor classified accountants with workers in finance occupations including bursars, operations officers, auditors, revenue agents, controllers, report analysts, rate analysts, credit and collection managers, risk and insurance managers, loan officers, securities traders, appraisers, grain brokers, budget analysts, and trust officers.

HELP WANTED

Accountant
One of the largest real estate service companies in the world has an immediate opportunity at our fast-paced Chicago loop office.

continued

> continued
>
> Candidate will be responsible for the preparation and review of monthly financial reporting packages, forecasting, budgeting, monitoring cash flow, coordination of accounts payable, and interfacing with clients. A bachelor's degree in accounting, one to two years of related experience, and Excel proficiency required. Strong analytical skills and the ability to work independently are essential. Please send resume.

WORKING CONDITIONS

Management accountants either have their own offices within a company or a cubicle or area in which they operate. They use computers and other necessary office equipment. Since management accountants are employed by private business or industry, they are more apt to work a standard 40-hour week than are public accountants.

HELP WANTED

Public Accountant
Fast-paced, multidimensional accounting department seeks self-motivated, detail-oriented individual to perform variety of functions utilizing in-house computer accounting system, accounting analysis, and reconciliation. B.A. in accounting plus minimum of two years' experience required.

TRAINING AND QUALIFICATIONS

High school students planning on embarking on an accounting career should take courses to prepare for college including mathematics, science, history, economics, public speaking, and English. Data processing or computer science is also helpful.

Most private businesses hire only college graduates. Students should plan to earn a minimum of a bachelor's degree. (Many firms prefer those with a master's degree). The major should be accounting, or business administration with a minor in accounting. Students planning on an accounting career should look carefully at college programs before enrolling.

For those interested in pursuing a specialized area of management accounting, perhaps financial planning and analysis, an M.B.A. is a necessity. Financial planners are concerned with the budgetary and financial needs of an organization—they investigate expenditures, profits, cash flow, and investments. They offer financial advice on the effects of mergers and corporate growth, and may have the power to reject or discourage major expenditures and investments.

The Institute of Management Accountants (IMA) confers the certified management accountant (CMA) designation upon college graduates who pass a four-part examination, agree to meet continuing education requirements, comply with standards of professional conduct, and have at least two years' work experience in management accounting. The CMA program is administered through the Institute of Certified Management Accountants, an affiliate of the IMA.

The Institute of Internal Auditors grants the designation certified internal auditor (CIA) to graduates of accredited colleges and universities who have had two years of experience in internal auditing and have passed a four-part examination. The Information Systems Audit and Control Association grants the designation certified information systems auditor to candidates who pass an examination and have had years of experience in auditing electronic data processing systems. The Bank Administrative Institute offers the certified bank auditor designation to candidates who meet its criteria. Multiple certification is permissible and encouraged.

In terms of personal abilities, accountants should be able to analyze, compare, and interpret facts and figures. They should have the ability to make sound judgments from this knowledge and be efficient problem solvers. Accountants should be able to concentrate for extended periods and be able communicators. Other qualities include reliability, accuracy, independence, responsibility, flexibility, and self-discipline. Accountants must work well with both people and business systems.

Most accountants today use computers routinely. With special software, accountants can summarize transactions in standard formats for financial analysis. These accounting packages are easy to learn and require few special computer skills. They reduce the amount of manual work usually associated with numbers and records. A personal computer allows accountants to use their clients' computer systems and to extract information from large mainframe computers. A growing number of accountants skilled in computer use develop software for accounting procedures and other purposes.

HELP WANTED

Accounting—Entry Level

Our office seeks an accounting graduate for an entry-level position. Responsibilities include all aspects of financial statement preparation. Experience is not required, but willingness to learn, be part of our team, and get excited are. New grads welcome to apply.

EARNINGS

According to a survey by the College Placement Council, in September 1994 offers to graduates with a bachelor's degree in accounting averaged about $28,500. Those with a master's degree received offers averaging $32,500 per year.

According to a salary survey conducted by Robert Half International, a staffing services firm specializing in accounting and finance, accountants and auditors with up to one year of experience earned between $23,000 and $35,500 in 1995. Those with one to three years of experience earned between $26,000 and $39,000. Senior accountants and auditors earned between $31,000 and $47,600; managers earned between $39,900 and $68,800; and directors of accounting and auditing earned between $50,300 and $84,500 a year. The variation in salaries reflects differences in location, level of education, and credentials.

Based on a survey by the Institute of Management Accountants, the average salary of IMA members was about $62,300 a year in 1994. IMA members who were certified public accountants averaged $68,500, while members who were certified management accountants averaged $67,000.

HELP WANTED

Senior Financial Analyst

Our radio station is seeking a detail-oriented professional to be responsible for weekly and monthly reporting requirements. This will include market share, weekly profit and loss statements, sports analysis, and accounts receivable. In addition, the professional will assist with tax packages, participate in the annual budget process, and complete other related duties as assigned. The qualified candidate will possess a B.A. in accounting and at least three years

continued

continued
of accounting experience, preferably in broadcasting or a related field. Must demonstrate strong analytical skills and work well under deadlines. For immediate consideration, send resume, salary history, and letter of interest.

CAREER OUTLOOK

Management accountants will take on greater advisory roles as they develop more sophisticated and flexible accounting systems, and focus more on analyzing operations rather than just providing financial data. Similarly, management will increasingly need internal auditors to develop new ways to discover and eliminate waste and fraud.

The outlook for the profession is good. Although the turnover in this occupation is low, the number of practitioners is high. Many openings arise as accountants retire or move into other occupations.

According to the *Jobs Rated Almanac,* accounting ranked as the sixth best overall occupation among 250 occupations, by the criteria of work environment, job security, stress, income, career outlook, and physical demands. As for job outlook, accounting ranked tenth overall—the above-average number of levels (sixteen) through which to climb, plentiful promotional opportunities, and changes in tax laws create work for these practitioners.

As the economy grows, firms and businesses will require more accountants to set up their books, prepare taxes, and offer management advice. Changes in legislation related to taxes, financial reporting, business investments, mergers, and other financial transactions require businesses to engage the services of accountants.

In spite of these opportunities, competition for the most prestigious jobs is keen. Job candidates with a master's degree in accounting or business administration, or a broad base of computer experience, will have an advantage.

HELP WANTED

Accountant
Full-time and per diem positions available. CPA with two to five years' recent public accounting experience needed. Audit accounting and tax experience required. Send resume with salary requirements.

STRATEGY FOR FINDING THE JOBS

The most common avenue for securing a position is still through college placement offices, so be sure to be knowledgeable about and take full advantage of what your college has to offer. Companies looking for accounting professionals often conduct campus interviews or prescreenings on campus.

Other avenues to pursue include state employment offices that list industry and business accounting and auditing jobs. Want ads in papers and trade journals often list numerous openings. In addition, job hunters may also seek out firms that offer accounting and auditing services. If there are no openings immediately, perhaps they will keep your resume on file in case an opening comes up.

Once you get to college, you should join several professional associations. As an association member, you will meet others who may help you find employment. Don't forget that networking is probably the most important route to landing a job. Tell everyone you come in contact with that you are (or will be) looking for a job. Perhaps they can put you in touch with a job possibility or with someone else who can give you the lead that will eventually materialize into a job.

PROFESSIONAL ASSOCIATIONS

Financial Accounting Foundation (FAF)
401 Merritt, #7
Norwalk, CT 06856

Financial Executives Institute (FEI)
P.O. Box 1938
10 Madison Avenue
Morristown, NJ 07960

Institute of Internal Auditors (IIA)
249 Maitland Avenue
Altamonte Springs, FL 32701

Institute of Management Accountants (IMA)
10 Paragon Drive
Montvale, NJ 07645

National Association of State Auditors, Comptrollers, and Treasurers
2401 Regency Road
Lexington, KY 40503

MEET TOPÉ OLUWOLÉ

Topé Oluwolé earned an Associate in Science degree in business administration (management concentration) and then went on to study computer science at both the University of Massachusetts and Northeastern University in Boston. He now serves as Management Accountant II at State Street Bank and Trust Company in Quincy, Massachusetts. He previously worked in customer service for the accounts payable department at Bolt, Beranek, and Newman, Inc. (in Cambridge, Massachusetts) in a temporary capacity.

"My work at Bolt, Beranek, and Newman taught me how different business and accounting cycles worked," he says. "I also learned how to solve problems that arose in different business scenarios. In another vein, I also felt that playing the computer game "Where in the World Is Carmen Sandiego?" was very valuable, although I didn't realize it at the time. I learned about world geography, flags, and currencies while trying to catch the bad guys. I also got to travel the world and learn about time zones without leaving home."

"I started my management accountant position in April of 1993. This was when I made the official change from temporary to permanent work. I came to work at State Street's international securities operations department as my fourth temporary position at the bank. I did computer work (Excel spreadsheets and Word projects) for the vice president of the department. Two major projects, the 'International Operating Model' and 'Request for Proposal,' introduced me to the concept of my future management accountant position.

"The 'International Operating Model' explained the flow of international securities transactions as they related to State Street and their international counterparts (their subcustodians). The 'Request for Proposal' explained to banks in the Americas, Europe, and Asia-Pacific region what qualities State Street was looking for in a subcustodian.

"At that time, I had just finished the computer science curriculums at the University of Massachusetts and Northeastern, respectively. However, I was faced with some serious cognitive dissonance. I wanted a career, but I also wanted a degree. So I faced the dilemma of full-time work versus full-time school.

continued

continued

When I was offered a permanent position at the bank, I told the hiring manager it would have to be nights because I planned on going back to school full-time. She said that was fine.

"I loved the international aspect of the business. To me, my job felt like a James Bond movie. I was the hero with a problem to solve, such as "Why is this account out of balance?" My problem usually involved contacting exotic countries like France, Sweden, Malaysia, or Singapore, if their bank was responsible. I had some cool weapons—a cash transaction system that international banks and I could browse simultaneously to reconcile cash discrepancies. And I worked mostly with women (a number of mothers who were working the second shift, from whom I learned a lot about life).

"I started working 3:00 P.M. to 9:00 P.M. but the workload was so heavy that I ended up leaving around 11:30 P.M. most of the time. Nine months later I switched to 4 P.M. to 12 A.M. There was no point working full-time hours for part-time benefits.

"The most hectic period was at the end of the month, because in essence I did a summary of the month's work in one day. My group had a mandatory overtime period of at least six hours in additional to our normal shift.

"Walking from the elevator to the department was like a scene from "Lou Grant" (the 1970s television show in which scores and scores of desks were packed together so tightly the workers could barely breathe). The daytime atmosphere was like an afternoon on the trading floor of the New York Stock Exchange—this is partially why I switched to nights. However, since there were fewer of us to finish the increasing workload, I had to survive back-to-back fast-paced, action-packed nights. I didn't know what a slow night was.

"My job involved booking daily transactions and reconciling balances of my subcustodian countries' accounts. Each accountant had a mixture of subcustodian countries based on their experience, the number of transactions the subcustodian had, and how hard it was to resolve cash discrepancies.

"Each subcustodian had a list of mutual funds it sold or bought into. Those funds had their securities. A subcustodian had anywhere from 4 to 400 funds. I made sure the funds

continued

continued

reported cleared and available cash balance (on the State Street international cash system) for any day was in line with what the subcustodian had on their books. If 94,000,000 Belgian francs on a cash statement showed up as 366,999 on the system, I had a lot of work to do.

"First I had to find out when the account went out of balance. Was it today? (Too easy, just look at today's transactions.) Was it last year? If so, I would have to backtrack to find the statement where the account was last in balance with the system. When I found the statement (not finding a discrepancy was never an option), I would proceed forward to pinpoint how the account went out of balance. Did the French subcustodian book a trade late? Did I forget to book interest? Did someone else who may have processed my subcustodian's statement book an amount incorrectly to the system? Did a broker dealing in Singapore dollars make a lot of bad trades? Was the mutual fund group at fault? Did the subcustodian make trades it did not send statements for? Every day was something different.

"I loved talking to my counterparts in Singapore and Japan. They were always so timely with the information I needed. It was funny explaining to a manager in France that my French wasn't that good, only to find out that the subcustodian had written in English, but with bad penmanship.

"I also loved experiencing culture and commerce in other parts of the world. Back then (before the World Wide Web boom), the average person didn't get that kind of global exposure in an eight-hour shift.

"What killed me was the sometimes erratic schedule. It was difficult leaving work at 2:30 A.M. when I had to be in economics class in six hours.

"To be successful, I've always believed you have to have a balance of real-world experience and conventional postsecondary education. If you're savvy enough to do them simultaneously as I did, then you will also be successful.

"Also, throw away the typical definition of accountant. Because of what I had been taught an accountant was, I swore I would never ever become one. I ended up in an accounting department by accident, but I wasn't the stereotypical bookkeeper. I was James Bond."

MEET BETTY FISHER

Betty Fisher earned her Associate in Science degree from Goldey Beacom College and a D.E. in accounting. She is now a consultant on staff at a company called Accounting with Computers in Pittsburgh, Pennsylvania.

"I took an accounting class in high school and it became like a game. I enjoyed it and took another accounting class the following year, and discovered that I did very well. I then went on to college for accounting," she says.

"My present job was attractive to me because it combined my accounting background with my management information systems (MIS) background," she says. "I install, train, implement, and troubleshoot accounting software. My job is to assist clients with conversions and upgrades. I create custom reports, fix problems when they occur, and teach customers how to use the software. It's busy, but at least I don't have the stress of covering payrolls and payroll taxes. I no longer have to worry about handling someone else's funds as I did when I was employed as a controller. The company I work for is a nicely mixed group where we all fit together like a fine machine.

"I like the creativity that the job offers. No one's accounting system works like anyone else's, and it's my job to get them up and running smoothly. It really is quite rewarding to watch the light shine in someone's face when they finally understand how it all fits together. The only downside is that the pay is not quite what I made as a controller.

"I think the best advice I can give to others considering entering this field is to be open and very flexible."

MEET KERRY L. BENNETT

Kerry L. Bennett earned a Bachelor of Science in business administration (emphasis in administrative management) in 1987. She also attended a number of training seminars. She is now on staff at Wausau Insurance Companies in Overland Park, Kansas, as a field auditor.

"My job is relatively busy. On a typical day, I start by leaving the house at 8:00 A.M. and going to a place of business to

continued

continued

conduct an audit. I will typically schedule two audits a day, which will usually get me home at 3:30 P.M. or so. I will then work at home until approximately 4:30 P.M.," she says.

"I usually work 40 hours a week. The work atmosphere depends on the location from which I am operating. It can be relaxed working at home, or more rigid at another place of business.

"The aspect I like most about my job is the ability to schedule my own work and the luxury of working at home (telecommuting). The aspect I like least is the feeling of not knowing many people I work with. Also, traveling can represent a substantial percentage of my job, so being away from home is definitely a downside. However, I enjoy working with numbers and people, and being able to control my own schedule.

"I would advise others to determine whether they would like going from place to place every day and then working at home. Some individuals find it difficult to maintain that kind of schedule. Be sure to weigh the pros and cons. Traveling for your job can be fun at first, but the fun wears off."

MEET KELLY HOLMES

Kelly Holmes earned a Bachelor of Arts degree in accounting from the University of Missouri—Columbia in 1989. She is a CPA and senior accounting manager at Coca-Cola Bottling Company of Mid-America in Leraxa, Kansas (a division of Coca-Cola Enterprises in Atlanta, Georgia). Previously, she spent three and a half years in public accounting at the offices of Ernst & Young.

"I am in middle management and spend a lot of time delegating projects and reviewing," she says. "My job requires a lot of operational knowledge of how the business works. I oversee general ledger cost accounting, inventory, fixed assets, capital, expenditures, and payroll.

"Of all aspects of the job, I most enjoy working with all levels of employees and the many departments who oversee other applications. My least favorite aspect is the lack of time to properly train sales employees about financial knowledge.

continued

continued

"I feel that understanding financial impact is a challenge. I'd advise all those interested in this career to educate themselves in the areas of public speaking (presentations), computer software, and financial analysis."

CHAPTER TWELVE

PATH 3: GOVERNMENT ACCOUNTING

"The legitimate object of government is to do for a community of people, whatever they need to have done, but cannot do at all, or cannot so well do for themselves, in their separate and individual capacities."

—Abraham Lincoln

Government accounting attracts those graduates and experienced accountants who want to use their management accounting skills in a different setting. Though government agencies tend to pay less than private industry, government positions offer distinct advantages, including job security, excellent benefits, and some unique opportunities. The goal of the accounting department of a typical government agency is to function within the budgetary constraints mandated by legislative action.

DEFINITION OF THE CAREER PATH

Many accountants, both CPAs and non-CPAs, are employed by a number of governmental agencies at federal, state, and local levels. Similar to public accounting and management accounting, these positions involve general accounting skills and specialization in more narrowly defined areas.

Government accountants and auditors perform a variety of duties, maintaining and examining the records of government agencies and auditing private businesses and individuals whose activities are subject to government regulations or taxation. This involves preparing the nation's budget, auditing public utilities, studying the background of bankruptcy, examining the books of stock exchange firms, and reviewing amounts spent by various governmental agencies.

They complete reports of examinations and, if appropriate, make arrangements to collect taxes due; ensure that proper forms are filed by the individuals or businesses; assess any penalties for nonconformance to government regulations; and advise when prosecution should be considered. Government accountants also examine the financial records of banking institutions and securities exchanges and brokers.

In a government department or agency, major concerns are budgets and grants. Since funds come from an appropriating source, requests must be detailed and precise. Accountants may be responsible for showing where matching funds will come from, exactly how a community stands to benefit, and statistics on the people it involves.

Accountants in government generally are called upon to take on significant responsibilities very early in their careers because of the enormous need for these services relative to the number of professionals available.

Opportunities at the Federal Level

Following are some of the numerous possibilities.

Financial Officer If you serve as financial officer in the administrative department of government at any level, your responsibilities may be as diverse as analyzing bonds and other sources of revenue, reorganizing inefficient bureaucratic procedures, helping to negotiate labor contracts and set up pension funds, and preparing budgets.

Revenue Officer In the capacity of tax collector, revenue officers collect delinquent taxes, investigate business situations, negotiate agreements in order to satisfy tax obligations, and perform other tasks to safeguard the government's interests. Sometimes a written civil service exam is required. Revenue officers then enter government employment at either GS-5 or GS-7 levels.

Securities Investigator The securities investigator is charged with examining books, records, and other financial aspects of national securities exchanges, investment advisors, and brokers, to determine their compliance with the law.

Internal Revenue Service Agents The IRS is the single largest employer of accountants in the United States. IRS agents examine and audit the accounting books and records of individuals, partnerships, fiduciaries, and corporations to determine their court federal tax liability. Following this, they prepare relevant technical reports and other work to assist the United States Attorney General in preparing the case and the trial. Candidates must have a four-year college degree in accounting, or three years' experience comparable to four years of college, or any equivalent combination of education and experience, or a CPA certificate. Those with experience only must take the written civil service test. Entry-level positions will be at the GS-5 or the GS-7 level. Candidates with college degrees will come in at the higher level.

Working as an IRS agent requires strong accounting abilities and the temperament to work with taxpayers. IRS agents may specialize in one particular area of this work. For example, they may deal exclusively with individuals or with corporations.

Accounting Clerks Accounting clerks (or bookkeepers) perform a variety of routine duties, including keeping journals and ledgers, preparing the payrolls, writing cash reports, and updating accounting forms. Accounting clerks must pass a written civil service test. Bookkeepers and accounting clerks are also employed at the state and local level.

Opportunities at the State Level

States also have a need for qualified financial advisers. CPAs in government have the opportunity to evaluate the efficiency of government departments and agencies. At the state level, a CPA may be a member of a team assessing the adequacy of the investment portfolio of the treasurer's office. Also at this level, government accountants may work for the Department of Audit and Control or the Department of Taxation and Finance as junior accountants, junior auditors, tax examiners, assistant accountants, assistant auditors, senior income tax examiners, or senior commodities tax examiners.

Opportunities at the Local Level

At the city and local government level, individuals may be employed as accountants, staff accountants, or accountant administrators.

Federal Job Opportunities—Open Competition Announcement

Accountant GS-0510-05/07 - BT7814

Agency announcement number: 97-223PA

Duty locations: Parkersburg, WV

For application information, call (304) 480-6164 or contact:

Bureau of the Public Debt
200 3rd Street
Room 206-1
Parkersburg, WV 26106-1328

Remarks: Promotion potential to GS-12. Announcement contains qualification requirement and ranking factors. Application must be postmarked by closing date. Some substitution of education or experience is permissible.

Department of the Treasury
Bureau of the Public Debt
Parkersburg, WV 26106-1328

Recruiting bulletin
Career opportunity: Accountant GS-0510-05/07
Promotion potential: GS-12
Amended eligibility requirement
Organization: Office of Public Debt Accounting
Division of Accounting Operations
Government Securities Management Branch
Duty Station: Parkersburg, WV Salary Range: GS-05: $20,459
GS-07: $25,341

For the GS-05: Additional requirements: None.
For the GS-07: Additional requirements: Specialized experience: Fifty-two weeks of experience equivalent to the GS-05 level that is directly related to the position to be filled and that has equipped the candidate with the particular knowledge, skills, and abilities to successfully perform the duties of the position.
Or education (include copy of transcript or a list of college courses including the number of credit hours earned to ensure proper credit): One full year of graduate-level education in either accounting or auditing or related fields, such as business administration, finance, or public administration; or superior academic achievement demonstrated through class standing, grade point average, or election to membership in a national scholastic honor society.

continued

continued

Some substitution of education for experience is permissible.
Eligibility requirements: Applicant must be a U.S. citizen.
Basis of ranking: Qualified applicants will be rated on how their experience relates to the following:

1. Ability to learn the application of professional accounting standards, practices, policies and procedures
2. Knowledge of computerized and manual accounting systems
3. Ability to interact effectively with others within and outside the organization
4. Ability to communicate effectively in writing
5. Ability to communicate effectively to present facts, ideas, and concepts

How to apply: In order to be considered, you must submit an application (optional Application for Federal Employment, OF-612; Application for Federal Employment, SF-171; resume).

You must enclose a copy of your college transcript or a list of college courses including the number of credit hours earned. If you are claiming five-point veteran preference, submit Certificate of Release or Discharge from Active Duty, DD-214, or other proof. If you are claiming ten-point veteran preference, submit Application for Ten-Point Veteran Preference, SF-15, along with the required proof. Complete application packages must be submitted (or postmarked) by date noted.

Bureau of the Public Debt
Employment and Classification Branch
200 Third Street, P.O. Box 1328
Parkersburg, WV 26106-1328

For additional information or an application package, call the Employment and Classification Branch, (304) 480-6127.

Hard of hearing and deaf individuals may obtain information via TDD (304) 480-7755.

Applications will not be returned. Candidates will not be solicited for further experience/education background data or for proof of veteran preference if the information provided is found to be inadequate or incomplete. Candidates will be notified of the results following selection by the hiring agency.

Equal employment opportunity: All candidates will be considered without discrimination for any non-merit reason such as race.

POSSIBLE JOB TITLES

Accountant

Accounting clerk

Accounting supervisor

Assistant accountant

Assistant auditor

Assistant controller

Auditor

Budget director

Certified public accountant

City finance manager

County treasurer

Controller

Financial officer

General Accounting Office (GAO) accountant

Internal Revenue Service (IRS) agent

Internal Revenue Service (IRS) tax auditor

Junior accountant

Junior auditor

Revenue officer

Securities and Exchange Commission (SEC) accountant

Securities investigator

Senior accountant

Senior commodities tax examiner

Senior income tax examiner

State treasurer

Tax examiner

Tax technician

POSSIBLE EMPLOYERS

The federal government system consists of 14 cabinet departments and over 100 independent agencies. These departments and agencies, which vary in size, have offices all over the world. The larger the agency, the more diverse the possibilities for accountants. The government departments that employ the largest numbers of accountants and auditors include the following. However, many other agencies and departments also employ government accountants.

Department of Agriculture

Department of Defense Audit Agencies

Department of the Army

Department of the Navy

Department of Energy	Department of Transportation
Department of Health and Human Services	General Accounting Office
Department of the Air Force	Treasury Department (includes the Internal Revenue Service)

For those who like to travel, government jobs offer abundant opportunities to relocate within the 50 states and throughout the world. Employment positions exist abroad for over 50,000 United States citizens.

Opportunities at state and local levels vary, but the greatest need for accountants is normally found in the larger departments and agencies, such as those handling transportation and road maintenance, law enforcement, and tax collection.

RELATED OCCUPATIONS

Related careers include financial planner, securities salesperson, credit manager, purchasing agent, bank officer or manager, programmer, statistician, marketing researcher, mathematicians, mathematics teacher, insurance salesperson, and managers of various types of businesses.

WORKING CONDITIONS

Accountants who work for government agencies generally work in well-lighted, air-conditioned, comfortable offices. They may have private offices or work in large office areas. They are usually supplied with computer terminals on which they produce their work. Those working in government agencies usually work between 35 and 40 hours per week. Working for certain government agencies, such as the Department of Defense, might require extensive national and international travel.

TRAINING AND QUALIFICATIONS

During high school, you should complete a college preparatory academic program including courses in English, mathematics, social studies, and the biological and physical sciences. Electives in business practices, accounting, economics, and data processing also should be included. Concentrate on building strengths in oral and written communications and in mathematics. If you take introductory accounting, you should understand that initially you will concentrate on fundamentals, not broad concepts.

A bachelor's degree in accounting or in business administration with a specialization in accounting is the recommended undergraduate program for persons planning on entering this profession. The federal government requires four years of college (including 24 semester hours in accounting or auditing) or an equivalent combination of education and experience for its beginning accounting and auditing positions. In addition to liberal arts courses in English, government, mathematics, the biological and physical sciences, psychology, and the humanities, students majoring in accounting normally complete courses in computer science, business finance, economics, and business law. Professional courses in your program should cover such areas as the organization of the profession; ethics and professional responsibilities; financial, managerial, and governmental accounting; auditing; and taxation.

Many colleges and universities offer master's degree programs in accounting. Some universities have a professional school or program of accounting that sets forth at least two years of preprofessional preparation and three years of progressively more advanced professional-level studies. While most states permit candidates to sit for the CPA examination upon earning a baccalaureate degree, several require college work beyond the baccalaureate degree.

Success as an accountant requires above-average intelligence, high mathematical aptitude, a liking for detailed work, and strong communication skills. You should have a logical, analytical approach to solving problems and be able to work without direct supervision. Accurate work habits, integrity, and ambition are important qualifications. You also should be able to make decisions and concentrate on a problem for long periods of time.

Accountants may be certified in one or more of five areas: certified public accountant (CPA), certified management accountant (CMA), certified internal auditor (CIA), certified information systems auditor (CISA), or accredited in accounting by the Accreditation Council for Accounting. Certification is available to accountants who have met the necessary educational and experience requirements and pass a series of examinations designed to measure their knowledge and understanding of the profession. Most states require persons who want to practice public accounting to earn the CPA designation. Certification assures accountants of professional recognition of competence and generally increases employment and advancement opportunities.

Government accounting requires extensive entry-level training. For example, individuals initially employed as IRS agents begin with an orientation and seven weeks of classroom training covering all aspects of tax law, fraud examination, and research techniques. Then, under the guidance of professionals, you continue your training on the job by reviewing simple taxpayer returns. Next, you receive classroom training on the examination of corporate tax returns and work with such returns. Finally, you are instructed in handling the more complex corporate returns, learning about tax shelters and other intricacies of tax law.

As you progress, you might remain a tax generalist, specialize in the returns of a particular industry, or be called upon to instruct new trainees. Investigations or special projects might also require your participation.

Federal Job Opportunities—Open Competition Announcement

Accountant GS-0510-07/09 BU1366

Agency announcement number: R5NP14-065DP-97
Duty locations: Redding, CA
For application information call personnel office at (916) 246-5351 or contact:

> USDA, Forest Service
> Shasta-Trinity N.F.
> 2400 Washington Avenue
> Redding, CA 96001

Remarks: Target Grade 09.
Duties: Performs professional accounting work.
Works in a team environment.
Duties include execution and administration of accounting and monitoring and reviewing expenditures.
Must be a U.S. citizen.
Permanent full-time position.
Salary: $25,341 or $31,000 per annum respectively.
Duties: At the target grade, the incumbent has responsibility for performing professional accounting work. This position is part of a forest team requiring the individual to work in a team environment. Incumbent must possess skill in communication techniques to:

1. Develop and maintain interpersonal relationships internally and externally to the agency

2. Promote an effective team atmosphere

3. Perform conflict resolution in a one-to-one and/or group situation

Duties may include execution and administration for accountability of funds; monitoring and reviewing expenditures; coordinating financial

continued

continued

reviews and performing audits. Analysis requires proficiency in using personal computers and familiarization with software packages such as Lotus, Quattro Pro, and Paradox. Knowledge of the principles, theories, and methodology of professional accounting systems to perform assignments independently. Knowledge of financial systems and authorities and knowledge of common accounting systems ensure accuracy of work and adherence to accepted principles. This includes the knowledge of sole proprietor, partnerships, and corporations for use in lieu of financial statement to verify gross revenue and asset basis (depreciation schedule). Knowledge of accounting terminology, codes, computer systems, and reports used in either program or administrative operations.

Call (916) 246-5262 for additional information.

Elastic requirements:

"A"

Degree: Accounting, or a degree in a related field such as business administration, finance, or public administration that included or was supplemented by 24 semester hours in accounting. The 24 hours may include up to six hours of credit in business law; or

"B"

Combination of education and experience—at least four years of experience in accounting, or an equivalent combination of accounting experience, college-level education, and training that provided professional accounting knowledge. The applicant's background must also include one of the following:

1. Twenty-four semester hours in accounting or auditing courses of appropriate type and quality. This can include up to six hours of business law

2. A certificate as certified public accountant or certified internal auditor, obtained through written examination

3. Completion of the requirements for a degree that included substantial coursework in accounting or auditing, (15 semester hours), but that does not fully satisfy the 24-semester hours requirement of paragraph "A" provided that

   • The applicant has successfully worked at the full-performance level in accounting, auditing, or a related field

   • A panel of at least two higher level professional accountants or auditors has determined that the applicant

continued

continued

has demonstrated a good knowledge of accounting and of related and underlying fields that equals in breadth, depth, currency, and level of advancement that is normally associated with successful completion of the four-year course of study described in paragraph "A"

- Except for literal nonconformance to the requirement of 24 semester hours in accounting, the applicant's education, training, and experience fully meet the specified requirements

In addition to the basic requirements, candidates for the GS-07 level must possess one year of specialized experience equivalent at the next lower grade or one year of graduate-level education or superior academic achievement.

Candidates for the GS-09 level must possess one year of specialized experience equivalent at the next lower grade or two years of progressively higher-level graduate education leading to a master's degree or equivalent graduate degree. Specialized experience is experience that equipped the applicant with the particular knowledge, skills, and abilities to perform successfully the duties of the position, and that is typically part of or related to the work of the position to be filled. Acceptable specialized experience may have been gained in progressively responsible accounting duties that show progression in the design, development, operation, or inspection of accounting systems; the prescription of accounting standards, policies, and requirements; the examination, analysis, and interpretation of accounting data, records, or reports; or the provision of accounting or financial management advice and assistance to management.

Note: Selectee will be required to provide proof of employment eligibility for employment in accordance with Immigration Reform and Control Act of 1986 (Public Law 99-603, dated November 6, 1986).

Voluntary experience: Credit will be given for unpaid experience or volunteer work such as community, cultural, social service, and professional association activities on the same basis as for paid experience. To receive credit, you must show the actual time spent in such activities.

Basis of rating:

No written test is required. Candidates will be evaluated based on experience, education (coursework and grade point average) and

continued

continued

training. Candidates need to emphasize any experience they might have that is directly related to the duties of the position so that they can be evaluated against the quality experience criterion.

Selectee will be covered under the federal employees health and life insurance programs and Federal Employees Retirement System (FERS).

How to apply:

1. Applicants may apply with a resume, optional Application for Federal Employment (Form OF-612) or any other written format of your choice. When preparing your application, be sure to describe any experience you might have that is directly related to the duties of this position as described in the announcement.

2. Copy of college transcripts or equivalent documentation of GPA and completed coursework. Official transcripts will be required for verification appointment.

3. Applicant supplemental sheet, (Demo Form 001). Completion of this form is voluntary and will not affect the processing of your application; however, all applicants are encouraged to complete the form.

4. Veterans preference: Those applicants claiming ten-point preference must also submit a DD-214 statement of military service, and an SF-15, claim for ten-point veterans preference. Applicants who claim five-point preference on service prior to October 15, 1976, will be required to submit a copy of their DD-214 at the time of appointment. Applicants claiming preference based on service performed after October 14, 1976, must specify on the application the campaign badge upon which they are basing their claim. A copy of the DD-214 will be required at the time of appointment.

We will not consider any additional information that is not submitted at the time you file your original application. Forms can be obtained at the address listed below.

Where to apply:

Shasta-Trinity National Forest
2400 Washington Avenue
Redding, CA 96001
Attn: Personnel Office (R5NP14-065DP-97)

continued

continued

All applications must be postmarked no later than the closing date. Candidates will be considered without regard to any nonmerit reason such as race, color, religion, sex, national origin, politics, marital status, physical handicap, age, or membership or nonmembership in an employee organization.

All male applicants born after December 31, 1959 will be required to confirm their Selective Service registration status if selected.

EARNINGS

Earnings of government workers at the federal level are somewhat lower than accountants in other areas. Government accountants begin with a GS-5 rating at $19,520, or a GS-7 rating at $24,178. Those with a master's degree or two or three years of experience would start at a GS-9 level, which pays $29,577 per year. Top earnings for a GS-9 accountant are $29,577 per year. Those with a GS-11 ranking earn $35,786. Salaries were slightly higher in selected areas where the prevailing local pay level was higher. You should also note that GS pay is adjusted geographically, and the majority of jobs pay a higher salary than those listed. When locality payments are included, pay rates in the continental United States are 4.8 percent to 11.5 percent higher. Pay rates outside the continental United States are 10 percent to 25 percent higher. Also, certain hard-to-fill jobs, usually in scientific, technical, and medical fields, may have higher starting salaries. Exact pay information can be found on position vacancy announcements.

Accountants employed by the federal government in nonsupervisory, supervisory, and managerial positions average about $52,00 a year; auditors average approximately $55,000.

Pay reform was implemented in 1990 to offset competitive hiring pressures from private industry and local governments. Agencies can now offer allowances and bonuses when recruiting and they are authorized to pay interview travel. There are also a number of special compensation systems that augment the general schedule.

All employees receive 10 paid holidays; and 13 days of vacation for the first three years, 20 days of vacation with 3 to 15 years' service, and 26 days after 15 years. Additionally, 13 sick days are accrued each year regardless of length of service. Military time counts toward benefits. If you have three years of military service, for example, you begin with four weeks of paid vacation and have accrued three years toward retirement.

CAREER OUTLOOK

Employment of accountants and auditors is expected to grow about as fast as the average for all occupations through the year 2005. Uncle Sam employs over 2,980,000 workers and hires an average of 35,000 new employees each year to replace workers who transfer to other federal or private jobs, retire, or stop working for other reasons. The United States government is the largest employer in the United States, hiring 2.5 percent of the nation's civilian workforce.

Recent changes make approaching the federal government far less intimidating than it was until very recently. Significant changes have been implemented to streamline the hiring process.

STRATEGY FOR FINDING THE JOBS

You must apply for government accounting jobs in the same way as you would for any government position. At the federal level, contact the nearest job information center for application details. Most federal applicants must go through the Office of Personnel Management, but some departments, such as the Department of Defense, have their own personnel offices. Look for most up-to-date information online. In either case, you must submit the standard federal application form, SF-171, and a college transcript. Normally, the federal government promotes from within, but occasionally openings appear that cannot be filled without looking for outside talent. Some agencies specifically recruit those with advanced degrees and/or work experience.

After your application is received, your qualifications are evaluated and you are given a numerical rating. When your number reaches the head of a list of qualified candidates for the position that interests you, you will be interviewed. If the job is in another part of the country and you are willing to relocate (always an important consideration when applying for federal work) you may be interviewed on the phone.

You may also call the Career America College Hotline at (900) 990-9200 (or in Alaska, call [912] 471-3755) for application information. Callers will be billed by their phone company at the rate of about 40 cents per minute. Callers first hear a list of topics, which leads to recordings that give current information about entry-level opportunities for specific job categories as well as general information on pay and benefits and how to apply for a job. Callers may also leave voice mail messages to request application forms and instructions. The system is available 24 hours a day, and requested materials are mailed the next work day.

Another possibility would be to write the Federal Employment Information Center (FEIC, formerly called FJIC) in the area you are seeking employment. Request the following information:

- Announcements for specific job series
- A list of local government agencies
- Application forms—also request a copy of the new OPM flyer titled *Applying for a Federal Job*

You may also accomplish some important research by visiting your local library and reviewing the following publications:

- *The United States Government Manual*—This book provides agency descriptions, addresses, contacts, and basic employment information.
- *The Federal Career Directory*—If your library doesn't have this publication, check with a local college placement office. This directory provides an agency description, lists typical entry-level positions, agency contacts, student employment programs, and so on.

Application requirements with smaller government bodies vary. Contact state, county, or local government personnel agencies to discover their needs for applicants.

PROFESSIONAL ASSOCIATIONS

Association of Government Accountants
601 Wythe Street
Alexandria, VA 22314

Internal Revenue Service
Human Resources Director
1111 Constitution Avenue NW
Washington, DC 20224

MEET BARRY FAISON

Barry C. Faison earned his B.S. in accounting from Virginia Commonwealth University in Richmond, Virginia in 1975 and

continued

continued

earned his M.S., also from Virginia Commonwealth, in business accounting in 1976. He also holds CPA and certified government financial manager (CGFM) credentials and currently serves as a controller for the Virginia Retirement System in Richmond, Virginia.

"I began my career working for the Commonwealth of Virginia's Auditor of Public Accounts in March 1976 during my last semester at VCU," he says. "At the time, certification as a CPA in Virginia involved passing the exam and having two years of auditing experience with a CPA firm or four years with a governmental auditing agency.

"My interest in accounting began as an interest in math," he says. During my first year and a half at VCU, starting in the summer of 1967, my major was math education (I had hoped to teach math). I left VCU in January 1969 to go into the Army, and spent the next three and a half years in the service. I returned to VCU in the fall of 1972 and changed my major to math (I had decided that I really didn't want to teach by that time).

"By the fall of 1973, I decided that I needed to have a more practical application for my interest in numbers and enrolled in an introductory accounting class. The class material and the instructor provided me the direction I needed to focus my interest.

"My father worked at a bank in Richmond for most of his career. My great uncle spent his career as a bookkeeper for a Richmond leather company. I think that these people influenced my initial interest in numbers and its related fields. However, it was my instructors at VCU who helped me finally decide on accounting as a career.

"I did not have any other related work experience before graduating from college. My first employment after college was with the Commonwealth of Virginia's Auditor of Public Accounts. This job gave me a variety of auditing experiences, including serving with a number of different agencies of the commonwealth and several other local governments.

"My last auditing assignment there led to landing my current position. During my previous assignment as one of the auditors on the audit of the Virginia Retirement System in 1978 to 1979, a number of weaknesses and problems were noted. Because of the condition of the records, a 'balance

continued

continued

sheet' audit was done and the report was issued with the audited balance sheet and a number of 'management points.' The Joint Legislative Audit and Review Commission (JLARC), an agency of the legislature, reviewed the agency operations and concluded that the agency should have additional 'professional' accounting staff and an internal audit department. I applied for and was hired to fill one of these positions.

"During approximately 20 years with the Virginia Retirement System, I have served as accounting supervisor, accounting manager, and the agency controller. In the span of that time, I have become accustomed to how most of the finance department works.

"My current position makes me responsible for three major departments within the System (member records, general ledger and financial reporting, and control). I spend most of my day either in meetings or working on a computer. Work in meetings involves problem resolution or planning. The computer work involves word processing—writing procedures and policies and general correspondence with participating employers and spreadsheets—designing forms, analyzing accounts, and preparing financial statements.

"The job involves having a number of different projects going on simultaneously. This means that tasks have to be evaluated and prioritized, and that sometimes there are more tasks than time. In a typical day, I spend a lot of my time dealing with exceptions. Unless I am involved in the installation of a new system or a special project, I do not usually work on the same thing two days in a row. The bulk of the record-keeping and reporting are delegated to staff who have responsibility for specific tasks.

"Routinely, I meet with the finance department managers and other department managers to coordinate current work and plan for process changes. I prepare spreadsheets analyzing the financial statement information and quarterly reports that include financial information from the general ledger, statistical information from the employer reporting and member records systems, and compliance information concerning the timeliness of reconciliations, employer reporting, and contributions payments. I represent the System in meetings with

continued

continued

other agencies of the Commonwealth on issues that relate to the interfaces with the System and/or new or revised requirements being proposed for the System. I am also responsible for working with the external auditors during their annual audit of the System. During the month of August, I am involved with the preparation of the financial section of the System's annual report and may work 50 to 60 hours each week, some of which is at home.

"The aspect of my work that I like most is the variety and flexibility. Because of my position, I am involved in all of the areas of the finance department and play a role in coordinating work with other departments. This allows me to do a number of different types of work each day. I like having the opportunity to be creative in developing solutions to financial recordkeeping and reporting problems. On the downside, routine administrative tasks are what I like least about my work.

"I suggest that anyone wanting to follow in my footsteps learn everything that they can. That means not only accounting and business-related topics, but other areas such as technology. It's important to learn how to use a computer, because you will have to use one in your work for word processing and spreadsheets. I'd also recommend that you learn a programming language, because the logical method of a computer program is helpful in developing organizational skills and the knowledge of programming makes it easier to talk to programmers and other information systems staff. Be sure to take advantage of every opportunity you have to further your education and to obtain professional certifications—advanced degrees and professional certifications may be the only thing that separates you from other candidates for a position. And never stop trying to improve and develop yourself and your knowledge base—most people don't remain with one employer for their entire career, either by choice or circumstance."

CHAPTER THIRTEEN

PATH 4: ACCOUNTING EDUCATION

"A teacher affects eternity; he can never tell where his influence stops."

—Henry Adams

Many first- or second-graders confess that they want to be teachers when they grow up. Some people arrive at this career decision a bit later in life. In some cases, it is the rewarding nature of the profession that is the attraction; for others it is the atmosphere, which is both stimulating and challenging. Still others enjoy the intellectual pursuits and professional stature afforded teachers. Many individuals feel they are making a contribution not only to the individuals they work with directly, but to society as a whole.

Certainly teaching has many rewards. But it can also be difficult, demanding work. And as a rule, most teachers will tell you that it wasn't monetary remuneration that prompted them to choose this career. Is teaching for you?

Ask yourself the following questions:

1. Is patience one of my virtues?

2. Do I enjoy working with people?

3. Am I confident about all the subject areas in my field?

4. Am I willing and able to put in the necessary hours? (Many hours are required for planning, grading papers, attending meetings, and remaining current in the field.)

5. Do I have the skills required to perform ably in front of a group?

6. Am I capable of maintaining discipline?

7. Do I have sufficient enthusiasm for teaching?

8. Am I creative enough to develop new approaches for students who learn in different ways?

9. Is an educational setting attractive to me?

Individuals who have been working in the accounting field are often drawn to this career because they desire to use their knowledge and accounting experience to educate others. As long as accounting and financial management practices continue to become more and more complicated, accounting students will require a stronger education to prepare for their careers.

HELP WANTED

Educator

The Department of Accounting and Finance at a state university is seeking candidates for a tenure-track position for next fall. Doctorate in accounting/A.B.D. (all but dissertation) candidates nearing completion may also be considered. Applicants will be judged on their potential for excellence in research and teaching, although preference will be given to applicants who can submit completed research. The college offers undergraduate and M.B.A. programs. Application review will begin immediately and continue until the position is filled. Please send your cover letter, resume, and names and addresses of three references to the Chairman of the Department of Accounting and Finance.

DEFINITION OF THE CAREER PATH

High School Teaching

Requirements for high school teachers vary from state to state, but everyone must earn a bachelor's degree from a college or university that has a state-approved curriculum. Graduation requirements include a prescribed course of study (usually including at least three accounting courses in addition to classes in management, marketing, economics, math, and data processing) and classroom experience as a student teacher, usually for a six-month period. Once you have completed your studies, most states require applicants to successfully pass a teacher certification competency examination. These tests are designed to measure subject matter mastery, basic skills, and teaching capabilities.

Some states allow you to teach at the high school level with a provisional certification immediately upon obtaining your accounting degree. Regular certification is attained by working with an experienced educator for one or two years while completing the necessary education courses. When certificates come up for renewal, additional coursework may be required. In some states, a master's degree may be mandatory.

As a teacher at the high school level, you may be employed by public or private institutions. Private schools are usually less stringent and often don't make state certification a requirement.

College Teaching

Accounting educators are on the faculty of community colleges, colleges of business administration, and graduate schools of business. A growing trend is toward the establishment of schools of professional accountancy similar to those of other professions such as architecture, law, and medicine.

Business and community colleges offer a two-year degree that usually includes introductory courses in accounting, financial accounting, cost accounting, and accounting for individual income taxes. Teachers conduct several classes per day or per week, give and grade tests, and counsel students.

Community colleges may be part of a university system. Teachers employed in a university system will find situations similar to those at a university, and their responsibilities may well include research and publishing. Qualifications for these positions include a four-year degree with a major in accounting (or a related subject) from an accredited university, and usually a master's degree as well. Often a CPA, doctorate, or other credentials are required.

All staff members are expected to excel in teaching, to work with students in both general and specialized accounting courses, to contribute to the profession through serving on educational and professional committees, and to conduct research and prepare materials based upon their research. Other responsibilities include planning and assessing course objectives and curriculums, preparing lesson materials, presenting classroom lectures, assigning and supervising student coursework and research projects, and evaluating student progress.

At colleges and universities, educators often begin their careers as instructors. After obtaining advanced education and/or experience, they may advance to assistant professors, associate professors, and eventually professors. For example, at four-year universities, associate professors have a minimum of three years of university-level teaching experience along with a doctorate degree.

An average teaching load is 12 to 16 hours per week, not counting preparation time, staff conferences, and meetings. Classes may consist of anything from large numbers of students in lecture halls to much smaller groups (especially at the graduate level) where more individual attention may be provided. Professors often have teaching assistants (usually Ph.D. candidates) whom they must observe, evaluate, and supervise. Students are usually required to turn in essays, term papers, and other written work, which educators must evaluate, grade, and return to students. In addition, teachers are expected to be available to advise students about career choices, courses, or other matters. This can translate into an additional three to six additional hours per week (usually slotted as office hours, where teachers make themselves available to students on a regular basis). Staff members may also be called on to aid in special projects, internships, graduate theses, and registration; serve on department and university committees; and develop proposals for research grants. Those who become department heads have additional responsibilities.

In addition to teaching, educators are usually expected to publish written work. Those who are employed at four-year institutions are expected to produce more than those who are on staff at community colleges. Teachers at community colleges are usually assigned a larger number of classes.

Accounting faculty are at the same time members of two professions—accounting and education. They bear the responsibilities and gain the rewards of both careers.

HELP WANTED

Educator

Our state university invites applications for one permanent, full-time (nine-month), tenure-track assistant professor of accounting position, which is anticipated to become available next year. Primary teaching interest should be financial accounting. The position requires a doctorate in accounting or A.B.D., an interest in and the ability to conduct research leading to publication, and the potential for successful teaching at both the undergraduate and graduate level. Six-hour teaching load, summer research support, competitive salary, and excellent fringe benefits are included. Send letter of application, resume, dissertation proposal or a research paper, and three letters of recommendation.

POSSIBLE JOB TITLES

Adjunct staff member

Assistant professor

Associate professor

Department chair

Department head

Instructor

Lecturer

Professor

Program chair

Teacher

University educator

HELP WANTED

Educator

Our university is an independent accredited institution. We serve about 5,000 students each year in undergraduate programs as well as maintaining an evening M.B.A. program. The accounting program has approximately 500 students and serves additional students who are enrolled in other majors.

Responsibilities include teaching, professional development, university service, and providing leadership to full-time and adjunct faculty in the area of accounting. Teaching assignments will include undergraduate and pre-M.B.A. courses in accounting and finance. Contract faculty teach three trimesters from September through early August annually. Both excellence in teaching and university service and leadership are stressed.

A master's degree in business administration or accounting, one or more relevant professional certifications (for example, CPA or CMA), recent relevant business, CFO or equivalent, and teaching experience at the undergraduate level are required. Ph.D. in accounting preferred. Applications will be reviewed upon receipt. Interested individuals should submit a letter of application, resume, and names of three references.

POSSIBLE EMPLOYERS

Teachers of accounting may find employment in public or private high schools, community or junior colleges, and public or private colleges and universities.

RELATED OCCUPATIONS

College and university faculty function both as teachers and researchers who communicate information and ideas. Related occupations include elementary and secondary school teachers, librarians, coaches, consultants, lobbyists, trainers, employee development specialists, and policy analysts.

HELP WANTED

Educator

Our small liberal arts international educational institution is in need of an additional accounting faculty member for next fall. Minimum requirement is an M.B.A. with a CPA. Terminal degree in business or related field is preferred. The candidate must have a commitment to teaching, interest in research, and international education. Faculty members are appointed for multiyear contract terms. Curriculum vitae with cover letter and copy of transcripts may be sent to the director of personnel. Applications will be taken until the position is filled.

WORKING CONDITIONS

Accountants teaching in colleges and universities have working conditions similar to other faculty members. They usually have offices in which they prepare teaching materials, study and write reports, do research, grade papers, write articles for publication, counsel students, and perform administrative duties. Schedules average anywhere from 30 to 50 hours per week.

TRAINING AND QUALIFICATIONS

Experts advise high school students to follow college preparatory programs that reflect as many courses in relevant business, accounting, and mathematics as possible.

Teaching at the college level requires a minimum of a master's degree, a credential that usually requires about two years of additional study beyond the bachelor's degree. During graduate school, students generally specialize in a particular area of accounting. If you plan on completing a master's or doctorate degree program, contact the graduate schools you are interested in for information on admission requirements so that you may plan your undergraduate program accordingly. Large numbers of doctorate-level educators will be found at four-year institutions. (Doctoral programs usually take four to seven years of full-time study beyond the bachelor's level to complete.)

A major step in the traditional academic career is the attainment of tenure. Newly hired faculty serve for a specific period (usually seven years) under year-to-year contracts. Their record of teaching, research, and overall contributions to the institution is then reviewed, and tenure is granted if the review is favorable and positions are available. Once an educator receives tenure, he or she is guaranteed a position on the faculty for life, unless there is a serious breach on his or her part.

HELP WANTED

Educator
Our Midwestern university is seeking to fill two positions in accounting. Rank is either at the assistant or associate professor level. Appointment begins next fall. A Ph.D. or D.B.A is required. Candidates for assistant professor must exhibit capacity for quality research and teaching. Candidates for associate professor must have an established record of excellence in research, teaching, and service on doctoral dissertation committees. Applications will be reviewed as they come in.

EARNINGS

Salaries vary according to faculty rank and the type of institution. In general, educators at four-year institutions earn more than those who teach at two-year schools and community colleges. According to a survey by the American Association of University Professors, salaries for full-time faculty average $46,300 (for nine-month contracts); department heads between $60,000 and $85,000; professors between $55,000 and $75,000; associate professors about $44,100; assistant professors between $34,000 and $39,000; and instructors, $26,000 to $28,000. Many faculty members earn additional income through consulting, teaching extra courses, conducting research, or writing for publications.

Benefits may include paid vacations and holidays, sick leave, health and life insurance coverage, and some type of retirement plan.

HELP WANTED

Educator

Southern university invites applications for two permanent faculty positions in accounting. Applicants at the associate or assistant ranks with teaching and research interests in tax and/or accounting information systems are preferred. Doctorate required. Professional certification desirable.

CAREER OUTLOOK

Accounting educators are in great demand today. Supplying the increased need for trained accountants in public accounting and industry has put a significant strain on the availability of educators in accounting departments.

Employment of secondary school teachers in general is expected to increase faster than the average for all occupations through the year 2005. Employment of college and university faculty is expected to increase about as fast as the average for all occupations through the same period, as enrollments in higher education increase. Other additional openings will become available as older faculty members retire. Faculty retirements are expected to increase significantly from the later 1990s through 2005, as a significant number of faculty members who entered the profession during the 1950s and 1960s reach retirement age.

HELP WANTED

Educator

Our College of Business Administration is seeking an accounting professor as a full-time faculty member. The applicant must demonstrate strong teaching qualifications and possess a Ph.D. with an emphasis in accounting. In addition to teaching, the successful candidate will assist in the implementation of an M.B.A. degree program and a major in accounting to be launched next year. Application deadline is next month. Send a letter of application, resume, transcripts, and three letters of reference.

HELP WANTED

Educator

Our College of Business is seeking a tenure-track assistant/associate professor of accounting. Teaching responsibilities include graduate courses in financial accounting and undergraduate accounting courses. Required: Ph.D. or D.B.A. in accounting (prefer degree in hand, dissertation defense scheduled soon considered). The position requires demonstrated ability in teaching and potential for service and research/creative activity. CPA or other professional certification and work experience in accounting preferred. The salary is from $55,000. To apply, send letter of application, addressing above qualifications with current vitae (including E-mail address), names, telephone numbers, and E-mail addresses of three professional/academic references. Include a one-page statement of your teaching philosophy, list of preferred teaching assignments, and service and research interests.

PROFESSIONAL ASSOCIATIONS

American Association of University Professors
1012 14th Street, NW
Washington, DC 20005

American Federation of Teachers
555 New Jersey Avenue, NW
Washington, DC 20001

Foundation of Accounting Education
530 Fifth Avenue, 5th Floor
New York, NY 10036

National Education Association
1201 16th Street
Washington, DC 20036

MEET JOHN A. TRACY

John A. Tracy earned his undergraduate degree at Creighton University in Omaha, Nebraska in 1956; his M.B.A. from the University of Wisconsin in 1960; and his Ph.D. from the University of Wisconsin in 1961. A licensed CPA in the state of Colorado, he currently serves as a professor of accounting at the College of Business Administration at the University of Colorado at Boulder. His book, *Accounting for Dummies,* published by IDG Books, is going into its second printing.

"After being a member of the business faculty at the University of California at Berkeley for four years, I joined the faculty at Colorado in 1965, where I have remained since," he says. "Actually it all began when I was tested in my freshman year at Iowa State University. The test results said I should be an accountant, which, to tell the truth, surprised me. So I transferred to Creighton University and majored in accounting. Subsequently, I went to work for Arthur Young and Company (now Ernst and Young), and then went on to graduate school. I have been teaching ever since. Coincidentally, I was recently asked to be retested as part of the update of the same test I took as a freshman. I still test out very high on the accounting scale. That might explain the fact that I have continued to enjoy this field and have never had any second thoughts about the career path I chose.

"Teaching university students for about 36 years has never been dull. From the student riots in my last year at Berkeley through today, the work has provided a never-ending challenge. Students, down deep, are still very much the same. I have not noticed any better or worse preparation in the students of today as compared with the 1960s students. I would make only one exception—I think that the students today might be a bit more spoiled, not always appreciating how hard their parents had to sacrifice to get to where they are today. I dislike seeing the students who do not work hard and think the world owes them a good living. The best aspect of the job are those students who appreciate the opportunities of a good education and make the most of their college years.

"I would advise others to work hard, stay in good health, and take advantage of what good luck comes your way. Further, I would recommend that you read at least one newspaper outside

continued

continued
your locale and work. And, above all else—learn how to listen to other people. Any fool can talk. Become a good listener!"

MEET JAY H. PRICE

Jay H. Price graduated from the University of Wisconsin in Madison with a Bachelor of Business Administration degree (B.B.A.) in accounting. He was employed at Arthur Andersen and Company in Chicago from 1949 until 1988 and retired as a partner. Presently, he serves as an executive professor of accounting at Utah State University in Logan, Utah, and a visiting professor of business at the University of Wisconsin in Madison, Wisconsin (both on a noncompensatory basis).

"I majored in accounting principally because of the results of Veterans-Administration–administered interest and aptitude tests," he says. "When I took them (right after World War II), I didn't know anything about the accounting profession (although I did keep books for school, church, and Army organizations).

"I entered public accounting rather than private accounting because it appeared to offer greater variety and a greater opportunity to serve a number of clients and companies.

"I began my career in 1949 when I was hired on the campus of the University of Wisconsin by Arthur Andersen and Company. I believed that Arthur Andersen was more progressive, innovative, client-oriented, and independent in its thinking than were the larger accounting firms at the time.

"As one advances in this field, the daily routine becomes more varied," he says. "In the years immediately prior to retirement, there was no typical day. Each day's activities could involve work with public utility clients, others in the firm, those in professional accounting organizations (such as AICPA), attorneys, engineers, and regulatory commissions. This would include telephone calls, conferences, meetings with clients and others, research on accounting and regulatory questions, oral and written presentations, expert testimony before regulatory commissions, and a host of other activities.

"My most favorite part of the job is the variety and intellectual challenge of the work, including the opportunity to work

continued

continued

with clients throughout the world. I found that almost all professionals with whom I had contact had high ethical standards. My least favorite part was never having enough time to study all of the material I felt I needed to know.

"My advice to others considering this field is to align yourself with your temperament and personality. For me, it involved becoming an expert in a specialized area (public utility accounting). This was possible because the Chicago office of Arthur Andersen had a large public utility practice. Others may have the temperament or geographic location to become more broad-based and less specialized.

"Ordinarily, a person interested in this field should be willing to continue to learn, to work long hours (more than 40 per week), to travel, and to accept assignments (short-term or long-term) any place in the world. Today's accountants must also be computer literate, and as a plus, be fluent in more than one language.

"I would highly recommend teaching, particularly as a postretirement career. It is a great means to maintain contact with faculty, others who are active in the public accounting profession, and especially students—who are young and vital and I believe far superior to those of my day. To be effective as a teacher, one must continue to keep up-to-date on professional pronouncements and business developments."

MEET RICHARD O. DAVIS

Richard O. Davis earned his B.S. in industrial management from Purdue University, West Lafayette, Indiana, in 1971 and earned a Juris Doctor from Fordham Law School in New York in 1975. He also earned an L.L.M. in taxation in 1993 from Georgetown University Law Center in Washington, DC, and achieved the status of CPA in Washington, DC, in 1981 and Virginia in 1982. He presently serves as Assistant Professor of Accounting at Susquehanna University.

"When I had nearly completed my L.L.M. in taxation (a necessary credential to teach tax or law at the university level,

continued

continued

in the absence of a Ph.D.), I interviewed at Susquehanna University. When it seemed like a good match from both sides, I received an offer and accepted.

"I had always enjoyed teaching, whether giving seminars or conducting training sessions. I started teaching tax and accounting at the university level in the Washington, D.C. area. This experience heightened my interest, and I decided to pursue the possibility of teaching full-time. I particularly enjoy working with young adults in the classroom and helping them make career decisions.

"I was attracted to the independence and flexibility that the profession offers. I had no false hopes that I would work less. In fact, I work just as hard now as I ever did. But I can choose to work when and where I want, subject to certain restrictions, like class schedules.

"I had previously worked for the federal government (IRS), a Big Six CPA firm, a law firm, and a publishing company. I had difficulty balancing work and family priorities at the CPA firm and law firm. At the publishing company, I got tired of writing about what everyone else was doing. So the teaching profession looked like a promising career in which I could still satisfy my desire for an intellectual challenge and a reasonable family life. I enjoy the diversity of life at the university level and the students help to keep me young.

"In the fall semester, I usually have a Monday-Wednesday-Friday teaching schedule. In the spring semester, I usually have a Tuesday-Thursday schedule. Teaching days are busy, sometimes hectic, but rarely stressful. I teach about 12 hours a week, but spend considerable time advising students and preparing for class. I also usually spend a good bit of time on university service, which includes committee meetings, recruiting, faculty meetings, workshops, and so on. I might average about 50 to 55 work hours per week. I also do some consulting for a Big Six accounting firm. Occasionally I am asked to testify as an expert witness in tax cases. In the summer, I spend time researching and writing. I also go to several professional conferences, examine my courses, and make adjustments.

"I like the flexibility to control my own life. Except for class schedules and office hours, I can plan my day as I wish. I can

continued

continued

do much of my work at home. This gives me a tremendous opportunity to be a major part of my children's lives. I have the obligation to do scholarly research and publish, but I have the academic's delight of choosing whatever I want. I do not have a boss looking over my shoulder all the time. I like working with students and having the opportunity to help them grow intellectually and to plan their futures.

"On the downside, I don't feel that professors are properly appreciated or understood by outsiders. We put in many more hours than people think. Accounting professors usually make more money than other professors, but the amount is still not terribly high. Sometimes it is hard to prioritize the demands of the job (teaching, scholarship, university service, professional service, community service). The tenure process is stressful. This is my sixth year (my tenure year), and if I don't get tenure, I will have to begin looking for another job. Also, it is sometimes frustrating when students don't seem interested in their studies.

"Remember that to operate at this level, you must have the academic credentials, especially since the competition for university professor positions is so stiff. You need a Ph.D., or if you want to teach tax law you need a law degree and an advanced degree in law. It's also paramount that you are a CPA and that you enjoy teaching. It's a good idea to start out by teaching in an adjunct position at a local university or community college. To help get such a job, network! Get to know as many academics as you can. It would be helpful if you could publish an article in an academic journal. A good publication record will help differentiate you from all the other applicants for a position. If you don't like to do research or write, you probably won't like being a professor."

MEET LELA D. "KITTY" PUMPHREY

Lela D. Pumphrey earned her Bachelor of Science-Bachelor of Business Administration (B.S.B.A.) degree from the University of Southern Mississippi, Hattiesburg, Mississippi in 1968; an M.B.A. from Arkansas State University, Jonesboro, Arkansas, in

continued

continued

1973; and a Ph.D. from the University of Missouri in Columbia, Missouri, in 1984. She has credentials as a CPA, CMA, CGFM, and CIA, and serves as a Professor of Accounting at Idaho State University in Pocatello, Idaho.

"After approximately 10 years of public accounting experience, I enrolled in a Ph.D. program to prepare myself to teach accounting at the collegiate level," she says. "After completion of my Ph.D., I taught at the University of Arkansas at Little Rock. I wanted to live in the intermountain West and moved to that area in 1988 when I was offered a position at Idaho State University.

"I majored in accounting in undergraduate school because I thoroughly enjoyed the subject. I found intellectual stimulation in the practical application of theoretical accounting. After graduation, I entered public accounting because it offered the opportunity to work for a variety of clients and gave me the opportunity to see a number of industries and specializations first-hand. When I entered the Ph.D. program in accounting, I specialized in the area of governmental accounting and auditing for numerous reasons. One reason was that I had many years of audit experience working with small governments and entities that receive federal funding. Another reason, and perhaps more important, was that I believe in the right of the people to know what their governmental officials are doing with the tax dollars entrusted to them. Public management and public policy are reflected in governmental financial statements.

"I had known since I was quite young that teaching was what I wanted to do. However, I was not sure what I wanted to teach. In college I was intellectually attracted to the study of accounting and I thoroughly enjoyed the practice of public accounting. Also, in high school I had considered a career in politics or law. Governmental accounting allows me to be associated with both of those topics.

"As a professor, I have no typical day. I am in the classroom nine hours a week and perform research every day. I spend a few hours each week consulting with governmental entities, and answering specific questions about accounting and financial reporting for governmental entities. Students ask questions and governmental accountants call and ask questions—both

continued

continued

require research. Sometimes students have difficulty applying the principles taught in the classroom, so I spend many hours trying to help them understand the principles. I enjoy students and I enjoy consulting with practicing accountants. Because I love my career, I work many hours, not because my employer requires them but because of the way I feel. I do quite a bit of professional development training for practicing accountants. This requires many hours in addition to my university responsibilities. I imagine I work 50 to 60 hours a week, by choice.

"My former students who are working for the state controller are currently engaged in preparing the State of Idaho Comprehensive Annual Financial Report. They call frequently with questions concerning accounting and financial reporting. They seem to be doing a lot of research on theoretical accounting issues. Also, they are interacting a lot with the various state departments as they attempt to identify accounting and financial reporting issues. Their work has included obtaining a state attorney general's opinion on whether a certain quasigovernmental entity is legally part of the state. I am also providing technical assistance to the state legislative auditor, who must audit the financial statements prepared by the state controller.

"I enjoy the challenge of communicating governmental accounting theory and of helping students understand not only governmental accounting, but also accounting in general. The challenge is also the downside—sometimes I fail to teach what I wanted to teach. It is frustrating to understand a broad area as well as I do and be unable to communicate the topic to someone else.

"I believe that there are many students who have no intention of entering governmental accounting but end up there for a variety of reasons, and then find it rewarding and fulfilling. I would advise anyone who is interested in teaching to first get some experience in the accounting profession and then enter a Ph.D. program to prepare for the research and teaching of their chosen topic. I am so glad that I had several years of public accounting experience. I learned so much in those years."

APPENDIX A

FEDERAL JOB INFORMATION CENTERS

Alabama

Southerland Building
806 Governors Drive, NW
Huntsville, AL 35801

Alaska

Federal Building & U.S.
Courthouse
701 C Street
P.O. Box 22
Anchorage, AK 99513

Arizona

522 North Central Avenue
Phoenix, AZ 85004

Arkansas

Federal Building, Room 1319
700 West Capitol Avenue
Little Rock, AR 72201

California

Linder Building
845 South Figueroa
Los Angeles, CA 90017

Federal Building
1029 J Street
Sacramento, CA 95814

880 Front Street
San Diego, CA 92188

525 Market Street, 24th Floor
San Francisco, CA 94105

Colorado

1845 Sherman Street
Denver, CO 80203

Connecticut

Federal Building, Room 717
450 Main Street
Hartford, CT 06103

Delaware

Federal Building
844 King Street
Wilmington, DE 19801

District of Columbia

1900 E Street, NW
Washington, DC 20415

Florida

1000 Brickell Avenue
Suite 660
Miami, FL 33131

80 North Hughey Avenue
Orlando, FL 32801

Georgia

Richard B. Russell Federal Building
75 Spring Street SW
Atlanta, GA 30303

Guam

238 O'Hara Street
Room 308
Agana, Guam 96910

Hawaii

Box 50028
300 Ala Moana Boulevard
Honolulu, HI 96850

Idaho

Federal Building
Box 035
550 West Fort Street
Boise, ID 83724

Illinois

Dirksen Building, Room 1322
219 South Dearborn Street
Chicago, IL 60604

Indiana

U.S. Courthouse & Federal
Building
46 East Ohio Street, Room 123
Indianapolis, IN 46204

Iowa

210 Walnut Street
Room 191
Des Moines, IA 50309

Kansas

120 Building
Room 101
120 South Market Street
Wichita, KS 67202

Kentucky

Federal Building
600 Federal Place
Louisville, KY 40202

Louisiana

Federal Building
610 South Street
Room 103
New Orleans, LA 70130

Maine

Federal Building
Room 611
Sewall Street & Western Avenue
Augusta, ME 04330

Maryland

Garmatz Federal Building
101 West Lombard Street
Baltimore, MD 21201

Massachusetts

3 Center Plaza
Boston, MA 02108

Michigan

477 Michigan Avenue
Room 595
Detroit, Ml 48226

Minnesota

Federal Building
Fort Snelling
Twin Cities, MN 55111

Mississippi

100 West Capital Street, Suite 102
Jackson, MS 39201

Missouri

Federal Building
Room 129
601 East Twelfth Street
Kansas City, MO 64106

300 Old Post Office Building
815 Olive Street
St. Louis, MO 63101

Montana

Federal Building & Courthouse
301 South Park, Room 153
Helena, MT 59601

Nebraska

U.S. Courthouse & Post Office
Building
Room 1014
215 North Seventeenth Street
Omaha, NE 68102

Nevada

Mill and South Virginia Streets
P.O. Box 3296
Reno, NV 89505

New Hampshire

Federal Building
Portsmouth, NH 03801

New Jersey

Federal Building
970 Broad Street
Newark, NJ 07102

New Mexico

Federal Building
421 Gold Avenue SW
Albuquerque, NM 87102

New York

590 Grand Concourse
Bronx, NY 10451

West Huron Street
Room 35
Buffalo, NY 14202

90-04 161st Street
Room 200
Jamaica, NY 11432

Federal Building
26 Federal Plaza
New York, NY 10278

Federal Building
100 South Clinton Street
Syracuse, NY 13260

North Carolina

Federal Building
310 New Bern Avenue
P.O. Box 25069
Raleigh, NC 27611

North Dakota

Federal Building
Room 202
657 Second Avenue N
Fargo, ND 58102

Ohio

Federal Building
1240 East Ninth Street
Cleveland, OH 44199

Oklahoma

200 Northwest Fifth Street
Oklahoma City, OK 73102

Oregon

Federal Building Lobby (North)
1220 Southwest Third Street
Portland, OR 97204

Pennsylvania

Federal Building
Room 168
Harrisburg, PA 17108

Federal Building
600 Arch Street
Philadelphia, PA 19106

Federal Building
1000 Liberty Avenue
Pittsburgh, PA 15222

Puerto Rico

Federico Degetau Federal Building
Carlos E. Chardon Street
Hato Rey, San Juan
Puerto Rico 00918

Rhode Island

Federal & Post Office Building
Room 310
Kennedy Plaza
Providence, RI 02903

South Carolina

Federal Building
334 Meeting Street
Charleston, SC 29403

South Dakota

Federal Building, Room 201
U.S. Courthouse
515 Ninth Street
Rapid City, SD 57701

Tennessee

100 North Main Building
Memphis, TN 38103

Texas

Room IC42
1100 Commerce Street
Dallas, TX 75242

Property Trust Building
Suite N302
2211 East Missouri Avenue
El Paso, TX 79903

702 Caroline Street
Houston, TX 77002

643 East Durango Boulevard
San Antonio, TX 78205

Utah

350 South Main Street
Room 484
Salt Lake City, UT 84101

Vermont

Federal Building
Room 614
P.O. Box 489

Elmwood Avenue & Pearl Street
Burlington, VT 05402

Virginia

Federal Building
Room 220
200 Granby Mall
Norfolk, VA 23510

Washington

Federal Building
915 Second Avenue
Seattle, WA 98174

West Virginia

Federal Building
500 Quarrier Street
Charleston, WV 25301

Wisconsin

Plankinton Building
Room 205
161 West Wisconsin Avenue
Milwaukee, WI 53203

Wyoming

2120 Capitol Avenue
Room 304
P.O. Box 967
Cheyenne, WY 82001

PROGRAM DESCRIPTIONS

THE BACHELORS AND MASTERS OF ACCOUNTING DEGREES FROM UTAH STATE UNIVERSITY SCHOOL OF ACCOUNTANCY

Utah State University offers an outstanding accounting education for the serious student seeking a successful career in professional accounting, business, or government.

The School of Accountancy enjoys a tradition of quality education. It is a member of the Federation of Schools of Accountancy (FSA), and is accredited by the American Assembly of Collegiate Schools of Business (AACSB).

The School of Accountancy has a competitive Master of Accounting program, with high standards of admission. The curriculum is frequently revised to keep pace with changes in the technical and business environment.

The profile of the Master of Accounting student at Utah State University includes:

- **Technical expertise** in business, computer applications, accounting, and taxation.

- **Communication skills** developed through personal and group presentations, team assignments, writing assignments, and class participation.

- **Human relations** or "people skills," including good professional etiquette and ethical conduct.

- **General education** in a broad curriculum, including a variety of courses outside accounting and business.

❑ **International perspective** achieved through a culturally diverse student body and a large percentage of American students who have lived abroad and speak a foreign language. International economic, business, and accounting issues are regularly addressed in coursework.

Requirements for a Master of Accounting

Entry Requirements

Applicants may apply for admission to the program during their senior year of undergraduate study. Accounting and non-accounting majors are encouraged to apply. Candidates are selected based on the combined consideration of their score on the Graduate Management Admissions Test (GMAT) and their grade point average from their previous 90 quarter hours. Generally, these must total 1150 using the following formula:

$$(200 \times GPA) + GMAT\ Score = 1150$$

Two Concentrations—Accounting and Taxation

To receive the Master of Accounting degree, a student must complete 45 quarter hours beyond the requirements for a bachelor's degree. Requirements for the bachelor's and master's degrees are as follows:

Bachelor of Accounting:

Fundamentals of Financial Accounting

Fundamentals of Managerial Accounting

Intermediate Accounting

Cost Accounting

Personal Income Tax

Corporate Income Tax

Governmental and Non-Business Accounting

Fundamentals of Information Systems

Fundamentals of Auditing

General Business Knowledge Required for AACSB Accredited Schools

General Education

Master of Accounting—Accounting Concentration:

Consolidated Financial Reporting, Partnership, Estate, and Trust, and Bankruptcy Accounting	4
Contemporary Managerial Accounting	4
Advanced Information Systems	4
Advanced Auditing	4
Accounting Theory	4
Accounting Elective	4
Report Writing	3
Electives (Corporate Income Tax and Governmental Accounting may be elected if not taken before; for USU accounting graduates, these 18 hours must all be non-accounting classes)	18
Total	**45**

Master of Accounting—Tax Concentration

Consolidated Financial Reporting, Partnership, Estate and Trust, and Bankruptcy Accounting	4
Tax Research and Procedures	4
Taxation of Corporations and Shareholders	4
Taxes and Financial Planning	4
Taxation of Partnerships, Estates, and Trusts	4
Tax Topics	4
Report Writing	3
Electives (Corporate Income Tax and Governmental Accounting may be elected if not taken before; for USU accounting graduates, these 18 hours must all be non-accounting classes)	18
Total	**45**

APPENDIX C

GRADUATE EDUCATION

McINTIRE SCHOOL OF COMMERCE AT THE UNIVERSITY OF VIRGINIA— GRADUATE EDUCATION

Today's accountants are expected to be business analysts and decision makers who bring their specialty—whether it be taxation, consulting, control, or auditing—to bear on corporate planning and strategy. The program seeks to cultivate in each candidate a sense of professionalism and an understanding of the dynamic environmental factors that are shaping the profession and contributing to the accountant's growing importance within the organization.

In recognition of the growing complexity of the accounting profession, many states now require 150 credit-hours of university education as a prerequisite for the CPA. The Master of Science in Accounting program at the McIntire School, which enjoys a national reputation, was one of the earliest responses to this requirement. It is an excellent preparation for careers in public accounting, corporate accounting, or government. For those interested in teaching accounting, the master's program provides excellent preparation for doctoral study.

Students enter the program with a firm grasp of business principles and concepts. Our core courses extend the breadth and depth of candidates' basic accounting and general business knowledge through advanced work in financial and managerial accounting theory, quantitative methods, and organizational behavior. Electives afford students the flexibility to design a program to meet their individual objectives, including the opportunity to specialize in one of four tracks—financial accounting and auditing, taxation, information systems, and financial management. Electives may be selected from the offerings of other schools of the university.

Each candidate's program must be approved by the Director of Graduate Studies or a graduate advisor. Prerequisite courses should be completed prior to enrolling in the program. Applicants who have not completed required courses are considered for special student status. The availability of these positions is limited. Students are chosen based on academic merit and outstanding GMAT scores. There is no foreign language requirement.

Requirements for M.S. in Accounting

Candidates must complete 30 graduate course credits. Nine credits of core courses are required, leaving up to 21 credits to be elected by the student. At least half of these 21 credits must be in accounting or taxation.

Required Courses (nine semester hours)

Financial Accounting Seminar

Managerial Accounting Seminar

Accounting Policy or Tax Research (for students specializing in tax)

Approved Elective Courses (21 semester hours; 6 hours must be non-accounting related)

Accounting, Tax and Legal Implications of International Business and Investment Transactions

Advanced Auditing

Advanced Accounting

Accounting for Non-business Organizations

Studies in Advanced Auditing

Special Topics

Taxation of Corporations and Their Shareholders

Corporate Reorganizations and Consolidated Returns

Family Financial and Tax Planning

Taxation of Partnerships and Their Partners

Tax Research

Professional Services Marketing

Management of Information Systems

Financial Controls and Systems

Financial Analysis

Investment Analysis and Portfolio Management

Contemporary Auditing Issues

Professional Practices Management

Federal Estate and Gift Taxation

Global Competition

Combined J.D./M.S. in Accounting Degree Program

Individuals admitted to the School of Law can earn both the J.D. and M.S. in Accounting degrees. Individuals must apply for admission to the McIntire School of Commerce in the usual manner. Commerce studies usually begin after one year in the School of Law. Students must meet all of the requirements specified by the respective schools. A student may receive up to twelve of the 86 credits for the J.D. degree by successful completion of graduate-level work in the School of Commerce. Similarly, a student may receive up to 6 of the 30 credits required for the M.S. degree by successful completion of coursework in the School of Law. Law students completing the M.S. programs also have the option to write a thesis for 6 credits, reducing the coursework requirement to 24 credits, 6 in the School of Law and 18 in Commerce.

ADDITIONAL RESOURCES

The Best Towns in America
Houghton Mifflin Co.
222 Berkeley Street
Boston, MA 02166

Career Information Center
Macmillan Publishing Group
866 Third Avenue
New York, NY 10022

Careers Encyclopedia
VGM Career Horizons
NTC/Contemporary Publishing Group
4255 West Touhy Avenue
Lincolnwood, IL 60646

Dictionary of Occupational Titles
U.S. Department of Labor
Employment and Training Administration
Distributed by Associated Book Publishers, Inc.
P.O. Box 5657
Scottsdale, AZ 86261

Directory of Directories
Gale Research Inc.
P.O. Box 33477
Detroit, MI 48232

Effective Answers to Interview Questions (video)
JIST Works, Inc.
720 North Park Avenue
Indianapolis, IN 46202

The Handbook of Private Schools
Porter Sargent Publishers, Inc.
11 Beacon Street
Suite 1400
Boston, MA 02108

How to Write a Winning Personal Statement for Graduate and Professional School
Peterson's
P.O. Box 2123
Princeton, NJ 08543

Index of Majors and Graduate Degrees
College Board Publications
P.O. Box 886
New York, NY 10101

National Center for Education Statistics
"America's Teachers: Profile of a Profession"
U.S. Department of Education
Office of Educational Research and Improvement
Washington, DC 20208

National Directory of Internships
National Society for Internships and Experiential Education
3509 Haworth Drive
Suite 207
Raleigh, NC 27609

National Teacher Exam
Educational Testing Service
P.O. Box 6051
Princeton, NJ 08541

Occupational Outlook Handbook
Occupational Outlook Quarterly
U.S. Department of Labor
Bureau of Labor Statistics
Washington, DC 20212

Peterson's Guide to Four-Year Colleges
Peterson's Guide to Independent Secondary Schools
Peterson's Guide to Two-Year Colleges
Peterson's Guide to Graduate Study
Peterson's Guides
P.O. Box 2123
Princeton, NJ 08543

What Can I Do With a Major In . . . ?
Abbott Press
P.O. Box 433
Ridgefield, NJ 07657

Where the Jobs Are: A Comprehensive Directory of 1,200 Journals Listing Career Opportunities
Garrett Park Press
P.O. Box 190
Garrett Park, MD 20896

INDEX

ABOUT THE AUTHOR

Jan Goldberg's love for the printed page began well before her second birthday. Regular visits to the book bindery where her grandfather worked produced a magic combination of sights and smells that she carries with her to this day.

Childhood was filled with composing poems and stories, reading books, and playing library. Elementary and high school included an assortment of contributions to school newspapers. While a full-time college student, Goldberg wrote extensively as part of her job responsibilities in the College of Business Administration at Roosevelt University in Chicago. After receiving a degree in elementary education, she was able to extend her love of reading and writing to her students.

Goldberg has written extensively in the occupations area for General Learning Corporation's *Career World Magazine,* as well as the *EEO Bimonthly* and other career publications produced by CASS Communications. She has also contributed to a number of projects for educational publishers, including Scott Foresman, Addison-Wesley, and Camp Fire Boys and Girls.

As a feature writer, Goldberg's work has appeared in *Parenting Magazine, Today's Chicago Woman, Opportunity Magazine, Chicago Parent, Correspondent, Opportunity Magazine, Successful Student, Complete Woman, North Shore Magazine,* and Pioneer Press newspapers. Her work has also appeared on an Arthur Andersen website.

In addition to *Great Jobs for Accounting Majors,* she is the author of: *Great Jobs for Theater Majors, On the Job: Real People Working in Communications, Great Jobs for Music Majors, Great Jobs for Computer Science Majors, Careers for Courageous People, Careers in Journalism* (Chinese edition published in Taiwan by Rock Publications), *Opportunities in Research and Development Careers, On the Job: Real People Working in Science,* and *Opportunities in Horticulture Careers,* all published by NTC/Contemporary Publishing Group.